A.A. IN PRISON
A MESSAGE OF HOPE

Alcoholics Anonymous World Services, Inc., New York, NY

A.A. IN PRISON: A MESSAGE OF HOPE

First printing, September 1991
Revised 2006
Fourteenth printing, April 2022

Retitled: March 2022
Formerly "**A.A. in Prison:** Inmate to Inmate"

This is A.A. General Service Conference-approved literature.

Mail Address:
Box 459, Grand Central Station
New York, NY 10163

www.aa.org

ISBN 978-1-934149-64-5

Printed in the United States of America.

4.5M – 4/22 (CM)

A.A. IN PRISON
A MESSAGE OF HOPE

Alcoholics Anonymous® is a fellowship
of people who share their experience,
strength and hope with each other that
they may solve their common problem and
help others to recover from alcoholism.

The only requirement for membership is a
desire to stop drinking. There are no dues or
fees for A.A. membership; we are self-
supporting through our own contributions.
A.A. is not allied with any sect, denomination,
politics, organization or institution; does not
wish to engage in any controversy,
neither endorses nor opposes any causes.
Our primary purpose is to stay sober and
help other alcoholics to achieve sobriety.

FOREWORD

The stories in the first edition of this book originally appeared in AA Grapevine, A.A.'s international monthly magazine. In this second edition we've updated the book by adding new stories—some from Grapevine and others sent directly to us from members. In this book members in custody tell their personal stories of the miracle of recovery. Each found freedom and hope from alcoholism's devastating disease through the program of Alcoholics Anonymous. These A.A.s share their experience with you in the hope you will identify with their problem, and that you gain the strength through the Twelve Steps, fellowship and tools of the A.A. program to join them on the road to recovery—physically, mentally and spiritually—from alcoholism. For more about A.A., you can read the Big Book, *Alcoholics Anonymous,* our basic text where you will find our program of recovery.

Perhaps our co-founder described this miracle best:

I have seen hundreds of families set their feet in the path that really goes somewhere; have seen the most impossible domestic situations righted; feuds and bitterness of all sorts wiped out. I have seen men come out of asylums and resume a vital place in the lives of their families and communities. There is scarcely any form of trouble and misery which has not been overcome among us.

Co-founder Bill W.
In "Bill's Story"
Alcoholics Anonymous, p. 15

CONTENTS

SLAY THE DRAGON

I had been a "guest" of New York State's Department of Corrections three times in three years. Each time they released me, I was never "ready to face the world." Far from it. Prison was no teacher to this A.A. My only "lesson plan" was feeling shame and dirty. That was normal to a victim of incest.

I first came into the Fellowship in 1988. I was 36 years old. I had no criminal record yet. I had felt I was an alcoholic after taking my first drink. After my first A.A. meeting, I could no longer deny it. I was grateful. I believed I had finally come home. The speaker at that meeting told my story. That was my first spiritual experience in the program.

With the speaker's help, I went to a treatment center the next day. I had no idea that treatment meant leaving my twin sons, age five. I would be gone for the next four months. If I had known that, I would not have gone. But as I look back, I think it was a very good thing that I didn't know.

With the help of A.A. and God's grace, I stayed sober for six years. My issues with incest were put on the back burner. The first five years, I ate, slept, and breathed A.A. It was the glue holding me together.

The sixth year, I decided to go to nursing school. I got very busy. I put school ahead of my sobriety. Then I got lost. A.A. became a part of my past.

While in nursing school, I began suffering extreme pain in my pelvis. A doctor prescribed a painkiller. (Of course, I never told the doctor my true medical history.) I fell in love with this drug. There is no other way to describe it. It made me smart. It gave me energy. It turned me into Super Mom. I graduated at the top of my class: a nurse at last!

My only focus was the drug: getting it, getting more of it, and making sure I had enough of it. In my first year as a nurse, I was arrested for forging prescriptions.

To us in A.A., insanity means "doing the same thing over and over while expecting different results." The first arrest got me probation. The second arrest got me boot camp prison with the New York State Department of Corrections. So did my third arrest. My fourth arrest was for felony DWI and parole violation. I was given a year at Albion Prison. All of this happened in less than three years. Talk about "self-will run riot."

During my years in prison, I lost my family. Both of my parents died, and my sisters and brother decided enough was enough. My sons were living their own lives. As a parolee, I was not allowed to live with them. That gave me another excuse to drink.

You can't scare an alcoholic—not this alcoholic. Getting "scared straight" was never an option. When I was released in 1999, I got drunk. I kept my appointment with my probation officer. When I got tested, I blew a .01, a violation. That could have sent me back to state prison. Instead, I received the grace of God and the help of A.A. I was in a treatment center the following morning.

This time around, I kept the focus on myself. I took the incest issues off the back burner. With the help of a very good woman, I boiled the hell out of them.

It was a walk through darkness and terror. I had stomach cramps. I vomited. I shook till my teeth hurt, but we kept going. The woman never let up. She would not give me a break. I cried and begged. I pleaded for a drink "just to get through the hard parts." I was denied time and again. I told her she was killing me, but we continued. I was hateful, but my anger did not sway her. The other women in the program couldn't deal with me. But I did not let their fear stop me.

I was given a book called *Strong in the Broken Places*. Night after night, I read and read. After weeks of this, my counselor held me in her arms. She whispered, "Carol, it is not your fault. But it is your responsibility." After that, I didn't want to quit anymore. I had freed myself of the demons. I knew I could never go back.

A mirror was pushed in front of my face. It held many images. But in the end, they all were good: I saw a woman of great strength and experience. It was a strength that delivered me from a childhood of the damned. I was a survivor of incest. A survivor of the New York State Department of Corrections. A woman ready and willing to face her life. To embrace it. A woman who could thank God for both the good and the bad things. They all had led to my awakening.

It's been nearly four years since my last prison term. A.A.'s Promises have come true, every single one of them. I recently got off parole and probation, but it was not a big deal. I know they were caused by my drinking.

My twin sons are both third-year college students. We get together often, and talk pretty much every day. God continues to keep them. I have a solid relationship with one sister, and a shaky relationship with another. My brother has chosen to stay outside my life.

My life partner turned out to be someone from the Fellowship. That was a pleasant surprise. It never could have happened if I hadn't gotten sober. We do not take it upon ourselves to keep each other sober. We are responsible for our own sobriety, and ask others for help during hard times. I call my sponsor and meet with her often. I have stayed friends with women I met when I first came in the program. I have new friends as well. A.A. has been my salvation. Sometimes I pinch myself, because my wildest dreams come true daily. I know I stay clean and sober because of God's grace, and the people in the program.

I am in contact with a woman who will be released from jail in March. I can give her only my experience, my strength, and my hope.

The hard times have not stopped. Difficulties, even tragedies, happen. Life on life's terms still sucks a lot of the time. People in the rooms support me, teach me, and love me. I still am stubborn. I still resent authority. And I still allow fear to get in my way. But it's okay. Help is in my heart and all around me. I simply have to reach out, and the hand of A.A. is there.

I go to meetings and share when I'm asked. I always speak about the incest in my story. I want to help women who hold on to their nightmares of abuse and shame. I share with them what's on the other side. I encourage them to face the pain, so they can let it go. I know they can find their strength and their goodness. I know they can share their hope.

A whisper for help brings me closer to God. My heart is filled with thanks and love for people everywhere. Together we will keep the Promises coming true. We will slay the dragons, and come to terms with life. The journey is filled with delight, with joy, and so much laughter. It is a great gift to know that we never have to be alone.

—Carol D., Homer, New York

SOUL SEARCHING

It was snowing very hard. The big snowflakes were all I could see through the bars at the Ossining Correctional Facility. I had been sentenced to 5 to 15 years. I was waiting to be sent up north to another maximum-security prison.

All my life I had tried to act like a tough guy. It kept me alive. But being around hardcore inmates, I knew I did not belong. I knew I had to survive. It would take plenty of push-ups and potatoes. Years of alcohol and homelessness had taken their toll on me.

As I sat in my cell, I wondered what had gone wrong in my life. I did not know about alcoholism. But I knew deep in my heart that alcohol had caused most of my problems.

A guard came to my cell. "You have a visitor," he said. Impossible. No one would travel up here in this weather. Especially, to see me! I had no self-worth, no self-esteem. But I would do anything to get out of my cell. So I did not argue with him.

I entered the visiting room. There I saw the look in my mother's eyes. It was the same look I had seen hundreds, maybe thousands of times before. Yet, this time, I had no

15

booze or drugs in me to ease the pain. I wanted to crawl underneath the nearest table. The only words I could say were, "Why did you have to travel in this blizzard? I can take care of myself!" I was still trying to prove how tough I was.

"I wanted to make sure you had cigarettes and coffee," she said with the love of a mother. There and then I knew something had to change. If I did not care about myself, I had to stop hurting those who still cared about me. But I didn't know how.

I was sent to Clinton Dannemora. There I got into more trouble trying to prove myself and survive. Eventually, I was transferred to a medium-security prison. A counselor named Bill L. took a liking to me. He was a friend of Bill W., and had been a member of Alcoholics Anonymous for 12 years. He read my rap sheet. He realized that I was an alcoholic who needed help. He did not inform me of my sickness. But he introduced me to A.A.'s program. He was very careful. I guess he did not want to scare me away.

I started working for him at the substance abuse program. But to do that, I had to agree to study for a G.E.D. He later convinced me to get into college. I was able to earn an associate's degree and a Juvenile Justice Certificate. I felt that was quite an accomplishment. I had dropped out of school in the sixth grade. But now I was beginning to feel good about myself.

One day Bill L. called me into his office and asked me for a favor. He wanted to know if I could set up the meeting room for some outside A.A. speakers. They might include some female speakers. "Of course!" I said without a second thought.

As it turned out, there were no females! I was disappointed. But I stayed and listened anyway. It was to be the turning point in my life, and my attitude toward life. The speaker was from Brooklyn, an African-American male, middle-aged. I also had grown up in Brooklyn. I'm Hispanic, and at the time I was in my late 20's. But I was able to relate to the speaker's every word. He described his alcoholism. He talked about his feelings of shame, guilt and loneliness. My God, I had felt these feelings all my life! But I could never describe them in this way. I could only act out through anger and rage. For the first time in my life, I understood my real problem. I felt a sense of hope.

I attended nearly every A.A. meeting from that day on. I was paroled at my first hearing—my first miracle. I was not expecting it because of my long rap sheet. I began making meetings right away on the outside. Through sponsoring others, I have learned the benefits of service in A.A. I have always wanted to become a substance abuse counselor. And through A.A., I have been able to achieve that goal.

But first and foremost, I am an alcoholic. I'm coming up on 16 years of sobriety. I am experiencing life beyond my wildest dreams. I could not have imagined the gifts I am receiving simply by staying sober. And by helping another sick and suffering alcoholic.

—Anonymous Male

DEAR MAC

Hello my friend. How are you? I hope all is well with you and your home group. First, let me say I'm great—praise God!

Mac, you can share my letter with the *Grapevine*. I can't keep my sobriety unless I give it away.

My past troubles have always been because of alcohol. I'm doing time for breaking and entering, and attempted robbery. I was really messed up. I was caught in the grip of a killer among men. I thank God to be alive today. I often cry a lot. I allowed alcohol to ruin my life. But the tears come from a mix of emotions: guilt, sadness, and joy. I know today I have a friend in A.A. The Fellowship wants to save me from this killer. It doesn't matter where I am. All I have to do is find an A.A. group. That way, I've found a friend. I really believe this today. I'm not afraid to reach out. I want to live.

For years I had been hurting myself. I had also hurt my family. I was a troubled young man. I hated my life and myself. I had no self-love or self-respect. And no love or respect for anyone else. I didn't know that then. Alcohol blinded me. But today I'm learning the truth about me.

It has come through the grace of my Higher Power and the A.A. program.

A single parent raised me. She did the best she could. But she had no skills as a mother. So I learned how to be a man in the streets. It warped my thinking. It twisted my view of life. And alcohol made the problem worse.

I've been in prison for five years now. I have 11 months to go before I'm released. I have had a lot of problems because of alcoholism. I didn't get arrested. I got rescued. And I mean that. I was death waiting to happen.

I had run-ins with the law. And I had been in jail before. But this time I hit rock bottom. I finally admitted it to myself: I can't use alcohol anywhere, anytime.

I still remember my first A.A. meeting in jail. I heard them say "Higher Power." They spoke about a "God of your understanding." Then someone said, "You can use anything as your Higher Power." I left crying like a baby. I was holding the Bible in my hand.

I didn't know it at the time. But God was going to save me through A.A. I didn't think that A.A. could help me. I thought those people were worse than me. That was my problem, even in jail: I was in sorry condition. But I didn't think I was that bad.

I read the Bible that night. My Higher Power led me to a passage that said: I can do all things through God who gives me strength. And I cried and prayed. Up to this point, I didn't know how I was going to make it. I was sad and tired.

I started attending A.A. meetings. I would sit and listen. I hoped that someone would say something to help me. To show me how to handle this monster. Week after week, I would hear the stories. At the end of the meetings someone would say, "Ask for help" and "Keep coming." I realized that was the answer. So I kept coming. Finally, my Higher Power helped me see: I have to ask for help. I've never been to a meeting on the outside. But I plan to go, God willing. Since being inside, I go to meetings whenever they have them.

I talked to my unit manager here about a Twelve Step program. She told me to suggest getting a program. To put it in writing. I did. It was approved a week and a half ago. So I'm waiting for that to start up.

Through the A.A. message, I'm learning to live "life on life's terms." I could never do that on my own. I'm not blaming others for my bad choices. I take the blame today. It's not easy. It's a learning process. I have embraced it in A.A. I want to live today.

I am grateful—truly grateful.

—Curtis

BRIEF HISTORY

Here is a rundown on my life of drinking.
I started drinking when I was 16 years old. That was "late"
in life. For that, I can thank neighbors who watched after
us. My mom and dad both drank. They had five kids. We
depended on welfare.
   I was called a "problem child." I would run away from
home. I ran from the abuse. I went through foster care until
I was 16.
   When I came back home, both of my parents were
drinking even more. They drank up the county checks. They
left it to churches, their friends, and our neighbors to feed us.
So I quit school. I got a job so my brothers and sister had food
to eat. Then I started stealing my parents' booze. I did it to
drown my feelings.
   At 18, I went to a rehab for 30 days. Before that, I had
been hospitalized. I had fallen off a third-floor porch. I
continued drinking. I had run-ins with the law. Then the
court ordered me to rehabs.
   At the age of 30, I was hospitalized with alcohol poisoning.
I had been to a Halloween party. I had drunk one and a half
fifths of Jack Daniels in less than 10 hours. I went home and
fell asleep in a chair. If I had gone to bed, I would not be
here today. My neighbor came to check on me. That saved
my life. I was rushed to the area hospital. I had my stomach
pumped and flushed. I was in terrible pain. I was nearly dead.
I had a high alcohol level in my blood. So they couldn't give
me painkillers. The poison shut my liver down for three
days. After weeks of treatment, I was sent home. I now have
hepatitis A and C. It's because of the damage I did to my liver.

This was a turning point in my life. By the grace of God, my life was saved.

I began attending A.A. meetings. I went for nearly five years. I had many slips. I went to a rehab for one year. Then I came to prison.

Over the 36 years before prison, I lost my wife. I lost everything I owned. This is the hardest way for an alcoholic to learn. But God had a reason. He took away my old way of living. He's given back my self-respect. I still can learn from my mistakes.

I want the time I have left on earth to be happy and joyful. By the grace of God, I hope to have that. I will be free someday. God willing, I can live without the booze. I want help so I can stop. So I will be a winner.

—Anonymous Male

MY NAME IS HELEN

My name is Helen, and I am an alcoholic. Like most of us, I found A.A. the hard way. I knew that I had a serious drinking problem. But it took me a year before I did something about it. By then, a man was dead. I was charged with second-degree murder. And I was in jail.

At first I thought, "It's too late now. Why not drink myself to death?" I had tried to die several times. Why not now?

But, by the grace of God, I am alive today. It must have been God's will. Living surely was not my will. I wanted to get out on bail for one reason: to get another bottle of Scotch and another bottle of sleeping pills. This time I would have "the good sense" not to call anyone for help.

My lawyer could see my sorry state of mind. He told my sisters. When I was set free on bond, a sister was there. She made sure I did not harm myself. I went to New York City to live with her. She has the same problem with alcohol that I do. At that time, neither of us would admit it. We began to have violent fights. Soon, I was ready to move out. Even if it meant going back to jail.

Instead, I found my own apartment. Living alone was a

gift from God. I was still drinking. But without extra stress, I drank a lot less. I spent the next few months thinking about myself. I wondered why I was where I was. I had always been active in my community. I had been respected. Then I had met a man, a heavy drinker. I started really hitting the booze. I blamed everything on that unhappy affair.

I went back to Florida in July. I began working on my case with my lawyer. The man I had lived with was dead. I was in serious trouble.

My lawyer sent me to an analyst. The first time I saw my shrink, he told me that I was an alcoholic. I went home and drank to that. Another time, I told the shrink how the man had abused me. He said, "No man could have done all those things to you. You let him do them."

Everywhere I turned, I was losing my excuses. I had to face the fact: I alone was responsible. That was hard. Every time I left my shrink, I had another drink.

Why should I quit drinking? I would darn sure have to quit when I was in prison. So why fight it now? Every time I got smashed, I wanted to down a bottle of sleeping pills. But I would remember the last time I overdosed: The tears running down my son's face. And how my daughter went to live with her father. She was tired of the misery at home.

My shrink was patient. He was always there for me. I think I quit drinking to make him feel better. I quit three months before my trial. I found that I could face my nightmare sober. It was still horrible. But at least I could manage the urge to kill myself.

Then I began to wonder: Could I face a normal life without drinking? What would I do at a party? All my friends drank. Well, most. I had several friends who were in A.A. I was living at the beach at this time. Everyone there was in a party mood. I started drinking tonic and lime without the booze. No one minded at all! I still had a nice time. I still had friends.

In fact, I had support from my drinking friends. My friends who didn't drink also helped me. They all cared. I began to trust my friends. I began to lean on them. It was the first time in my life. And not one turned a cold shoulder.

I began to have long talks with my A.A. friends. They were there for me 24 hours a day. Finally, one of them talked me into going to a meeting. I really went to get her off my back. Again, I was surprised at the warmth and care I found there. Some of them knew I was waiting to go on trial for murder. But they still showed they cared.

I began to find out important things: All my life, I was the one who had pushed people away. I had lied to myself and everyone else. I learned that people really did like me. They weren't all after something. Now I had nothing to give but myself.

I was tried and convicted of manslaughter. I went to prison. I'm still there now. I was feeling a lot of fear, guilt, and no hope. Then I joined the prison A.A. group. I found moral support from the visiting speakers. But I still didn't believe them when they said, "Things will get better. Turn your troubles over to God."

How could God help me where I was? He wasn't going to get me out of prison. He would not hush the 80 women in this dorm so I could sleep at night. Or keep them from stealing and swearing and fighting. God may be everywhere, but I surely did not see Him in here!

Then I began to give in to my situation. I kept going to A.A. and to church. I was hoping for something—not really sure what. Then I did begin to feel a little better. I began to smile from time to time. I even began to feel kinder toward the awful animals in here. Then I found out something amazing: These "animals" had names—and feelings—and fears—just like me! I began to comfort some of them. I began to advise them. And I forgot about myself for a while. Helping them helped me.

One day, I needed to write a letter. I said that I was almost out of paper. Suddenly, I had enough paper to write a book! Three or four inmates came to me. They gave me sheets of paper from their own supply. I had been blind. I had not seen my friends. They had been there knocking at the door. And I had been afraid to answer. At last, I opened the door.

Things are looking up now. My friends in here comfort me. My friends from the outside do what they can, too. I am learning to live as A.A. suggests. I live in the Twelve Steps. It makes life better for me. And for those who live with me.

I am growing in ways I needed to grow. When I leave this place, I will be strong enough to survive. Thanks to God, A.A., church, a loving family, and my friends. I am going to make it now—one day at a time.

—H.P., Florida

NO LONGER
A PHONY

Two words kept jumping out at me from Chapter Five in the Big Book: "rigorous honesty." Chapter Five speaks of honesty three times on the first page. But why is "rigorous" thrown in?

After I got in A.A., I kept trying to work the program. I tried working that Fourth Step. At last I understood: To succeed in this program, I had to be honest with myself. Without honesty, I can't work the Steps. I can't work the program. I can't stay sober.

To show how this has affected my life, I'd like to share an experience. It's about my time with other inmates in A.A. and others who are thinking about joining a group. In prison, we have an unwritten code. It constantly affects our everyday decisions. Every day, a person faces a choice: Will I be honest or not?

I work here as a draftsman. I help prepare plans for constructing buildings. I have access to art supplies. I needed to find some means of support. I decided to design and sell greeting cards. It was a "hobby" for profit.

What better position could I be in? I could buy a few low-cost supplies. We have to, if we want to do art work in the cell. I could take the other supplies while I was on the job. I did a good job for them all day, five days a week. So why shouldn't I "borrow" a few supplies?

At about the same time, I got "political" in the A.A. program here. (I was phony as a three-dollar bill at this point.) I hustled enough support and votes to win the secretary's spot. I was a big shot in one of the largest A.A. groups in the Texas Department of Corrections.

Then the monkey wrench got thrown into the old machine. I decided to start reading the books about the program. I did it because I didn't want to be embarrassed. I was afraid someone might ask me questions I could not answer.

Well, most of you A.A.s know the rest of the story—I got hooked on the program! And the battle with my conscience began.

I fought with my inner self day and night. Here I stood on Sundays, in front of more than 200 inmates. I would tell them that A.A. was an honest program. But I couldn't get honest with myself.

I can't put my finger on exactly when it hit me. But it did. I unloaded every piece of stolen goods I had in my house (my cell). We talk about getting rid of that heavy load we carry on our shoulders. Well, I did. I became 10,000 pounds lighter at the moment of truth.

I wanted to go out and tell the world all about it. I went to three or four of my close friends in the A.A. program. I told them about what had happened and how great it felt. No one in prison accepts things at face value. They thought this was a phase I was going through. Knowing what a phony I had been, I sure couldn't blame them.

I don't know if this was my spiritual awakening. But I do know my life has changed for the better. I am more pleased with myself and others. I work the program with more "rigorous honesty" than ever before.

In closing, I want to say this to any newcomers to prison A.A. programs: The meat of the program is the Alcoholics Anonymous Big Book. Pick this book up and read it from cover to cover. You'll be glad you did.

—Stan, Texas

THE ONE PRAYER THAT REALLY MATTERED

All my life, I had said many prayers. Most of them went something like this: "Please God, get me out of this jam! And I promise to be good!"

Each time they shoved me in the back of a police car, I prayed. Each time the metal door in the cellblock slammed, I prayed. Each time I stood in front of the judge, I said, "God, I will never do wrong again." I meant it too. That's the sad thing. I honestly wanted to stay out of trouble. But I did not see the real problem: Me.

I began drinking and doing drugs at the age of 11. At first, I did it to fit in. Then I tried to escape feelings of loneliness and less-than. I had felt like that as long as I could remember. This led me to hurt others, and hurt myself. Those actions brought on guilt and shame. Then I drank to escape those feelings.

This progressed, as alcoholism always does: I was drinking and using every single day. I found myself living on skid row. By now, I was drinking to stay alive. I was 31 years old. I didn't know any other way to live. I had a huge hole in my soul. I could no longer imagine life with or without alcohol. I was at the jumping-off place: the place that the Big Book talks about in "A Vision for You."

Early one morning, I was alone in a hotel room. The pain was too much for me. I was crying and I sank to my knees. My prayer was simple: "God, I can't go on like this. I don't know how else to live. Please help." I still kept drinking and using. But I believe that prayer was my surrender. Two weeks later, my Higher Power answered my prayer. The answer came in the form of the city's finest—the Honolulu Police Department. I was arrested once again. And off to jail I went.

But this time it was different. There was a change deep within me. I had a more open mind. I was going to do two years in prison as a repeat offender. I applied for treatment "classes." I wanted to look good for the Parole Board. But I also started going to the prison's A.A. meetings. I brought my paper along so the secretary could sign it. By the grace of my Higher Power, this started my recovery. It was my return from a hopeless state of mind and body.

The supervisor of my treatment classes was a member of Alcoholics Anonymous. We met three mornings a week. She would share her experience, strength and hope with us. She was a lot different from me. Her bottom involved falling off barstools in high-class clubs. She slept with a few strangers. I could not relate at all. And then she started talking about her feelings. How she felt lonely and less-than. How she felt angry and afraid. She could have been talking about me! She also shared about her life being sober. She spoke of the beauty of recovery. I began to have some hope.

Many prisoners used the A.A. meetings to hook up with their girlfriends. The women lived in other housing. So at times, I didn't want to go to meetings. There was a lot of cross talk and arguments. But I started really listening to the readings. I listened closely to "How It Works." I even offered to read sometimes.

One night we had an outside speaker. It was a woman

about my age. She told a story that was a lot like mine. She talked about the confusion and depression in her life. She talked about what happened that changed her life. And she shared the miracle of her life today. I felt another seed of hope planted. I started praying each night. I used the Serenity and Third Step Prayers. At first, I couldn't remember all the words. So I wrote them on a little piece of paper. Then I read them over and over. At last, I could remember them. I also read the Big Book, especially the stories. I began to see that I was an alcoholic.

After four months, I was released to a state work program. I would be there instead of in prison. I was scared to death. In the past, every time I got out, I would do the same thing— go right back to my old hangouts. But this time, I found a meeting close by. I started attending on a daily basis. I knew this: If I didn't begin to work the A.A. program, I would not stick around. My Higher Power knows just what I need. Angels were placed in my path. They showed me that this program really works. It has been four years, three months and 27 days since I walked out of those prison gates. I have never had to go back. I haven't had a drink or drug in that time. I have not hurt anyone on purpose, even myself.

In the beginning, I heard someone say, "If you want what we have, then do what we do." I took that to heart. I know how to drink, steal, lie, and cheat. I know how to use people, and how to let people down. I don't know how to live life. Here was a group of people who were staying sober. They were learning how to live life on life's terms. I joined a home group. I got a sponsor. I began working the Twelve Steps. I began doing service. And, no matter what, I didn't drink.

Today, I am becoming a woman I never thought I could be. I have a job. I also go to college part-time. I'm mending my relationships with my family, especially with my daughter. I had abandoned her 13 years ago; I couldn't take care of her. I am learning how to be a friend among friends, a worker among workers. Most of all, I am a grateful member of Alcoholics Anonymous.

This is my message to anyone who is struggling out there: If I can change, then anyone can!

—Elizabeth B., Honolulu, Hawaii

SCHOOL OF
HARD KNOCKS

When I was younger, I heard someone in an Alcoholics Anonymous meeting say this: "I judged myself based on my intentions. But the world always judged me on my actions." At the time, I was too young to understand that statement. But one day, I would see how it affected my life.

I was a teenager back then. I had a few days in A.A. I thought that I had it so rough. There was not a thing that anyone could tell me about drinking. With that kind of thinking, I lived a few more years in misery. Without A.A., I cannot tell you where I'd be today. It has taken hard work with honest sponsors. It has taken a year in prison. But I am starting to see myself: who I was, and who I really am.

I was a liar, cheat and thief when I was five years old. I was stealing and lying before I even knew what the words meant. By the age of 15, I could control just about anyone. I believed my own lies. As an adult, my behavior only got worse. To my family and everyone around me, I may have seemed like I was enjoying myself. But inside, I felt bad about my behavior. Still, I didn't know how else to act.

When I was 10, I began stealing alcohol from everyone.

I would drink it like it was my last drink. I always wanted more. And I would go to any length for the drink. Or the thrill connected with the drink.

On my 21st birthday, I got a job in a gentlemen's club in Washington, D.C. I could not wait to begin working there. Now my drinking was at a new level. So were my drunken actions. It wasn't long before I was fired from every club in D.C. Drinking was costing me jobs. It was ruining my relationships. And I was spending a huge amount of money. I felt shame about my lifestyle. But I never saw a way out of it. At this point, I was separated from my family. They would get visits from police detectives trying to find me.

To support my heavy habit, I committed crimes on a daily basis. I began to burn out. It wasn't long before I was arrested in Virginia. I received a date to appear in court. Then I fled to California. I did not know where I would go, but I knew I had to do something different. I know this sounds crazy, but in California, I began to notice a whole new way of life. It was a life I never thought about while I was drunk. Now I thought that I could be a part of it.

So there I was in sunny California. I was 3,000 miles away from the mess I had made of my life. But I still knew that I was a fugitive. That made me very nervous. I had a hard time getting along with people. I just couldn't trust anyone. I wanted to get sober. But I was filled with fear. I couldn't even share with a sponsor. In Southern California, I checked into a halfway house for women. I put together a few sober months. That was just by going to meetings. But before I knew it, I was drunk again.

Weeks went by. I was drinking like I had never stopped. Within days, I went back to the same old criminal actions. I thought I had left them behind in Maryland.

Then something changed. On the morning of April 3, 1999, I lay there, passed out. Then, as I came to, I suddenly saw the truth: I am powerless over alcohol. And it makes my life unmanageable. On this morning, I found out I had been trying to run from the disease. And the disease had followed me. I knew then what I know today: I am an alcoholic.

I really began to work the program of Alcoholics Anonymous. The way it is outlined in the Big Book and in the Twelve Steps and Twelve Traditions. My Higher Power seemed to know what I needed: a really tough sponsor. Luckily, there were a lot of them in Santa Barbara, California. My sponsor led me into the Steps. She led me into action. And she helped me get right with my Higher Power.

With the support of my family, A.A. and my Higher Power, I went back to Virginia. I turned myself in. I had just celebrated one year of sobriety. I had a few other warrants to clear up in Maryland. The judge in Virginia allowed me to go to Maryland and surrender there too.

One of the Maryland warrants was for a robbery I committed while I was drunk. I also assaulted a clerk and stole $400. I knew I needed to make a direct amends to the clerk. I did what the courts would allow: I wrote a letter. I paid back the money that I stole. I was sentenced to 10 years in prison. I was to serve two years. I was released after one year, with three years probation.

I needed prison to teach me lessons: about compassion and humility. I had been unwilling to learn them anywhere else. I never want to go back to prison. But the experience taught me so much about myself. I stayed sober while in prison. I worked with other alcoholics. I made new sober contacts. One day at a time, I have stayed sober after prison. How? By doing the same things I did before I went there.

I have just celebrated five years of sobriety. I continue to work the Steps. To be of service to my fellows. And to practice A.A.'s principles in all my daily affairs.

The miracles just keep on coming. I am a student at the local university, majoring in paralegal studies. I co-own a store where we sell books and gifts. I manage a recovery club; we hold Twelve Step meetings throughout the day. I used to expect praise for all of these wonderful things that I do. But the praise belongs to my Higher Power and to Alcoholics Anonymous. I once was a drunk who stole, hurt people, and hurt myself. Today, my actions consist of service and gratitude.

—Anonymous Female

SUDDENLY THE PROGRAM CAME ALIVE

I have been around A.A. for about nine years. I don't remember my first meeting. But I do know that I had a problem with booze.

At age 15, booze already meant more than my life. One night my high school sweetheart threw my bottle out the car window. I hopped out to get it. I didn't stop to think that we were on an expressway. We were traveling about 50 miles an hour. I paid for the bottle with a broken leg and a concussion. I was laid up for six months. At the time, I didn't think drinking was affecting my life. Now, I can see that my drinking kept getting worse. And so did my problems.

I was only 13 when I started drinking. At 15, it was already taking a heavy toll on my body. At 16, I started getting in trouble with the local police. I was known as a nice kid. But when I drank, I became a kid with a problem.

I hated to sit at home. I was out in gin mills daily. I ended up in strange places at weird hours. Often with the police right behind me. I might get an urge for some egg drop soup at 2 a.m. I would find myself at the Chinese restaurant. I'd be in the kitchen, cooking. More often than not, the police would find me bleeding from cuts. I had walked through the restaurant's glass window or door. The police call this breaking and entering.

I had another illegal habit: I might need a drink when the bars were closed. I would smash the window of a liquor store. I would help myself to a bottle or two. The police called this burglary.

After about six arrests, the courts felt I should do time. I was sentenced to three years in an upstate New York prison. When I got there, I saw a lot of people from my neighborhood. It didn't register with me then: I had a very narrow circle of friends.

While in prison, I did my thing: I drank daily. I had a good job. It allowed me to make as much jailhouse booze as I needed. I did two years of my sentence. I came out no wiser than when I went in.

Somehow, I found out about A.A. I figured I would give it a shot. The people I met at the meeting were really nice. I liked what they had to say. I liked the way they said it. But I was not ready to throw in the towel. I felt I had a few more good times left. For the next few years, I bounced in and out of A.A. like a rubber ball. When I was hurting, I would go to meetings and get dry, but not sober. I would use the parts of the program I liked. When things looked brighter, I would leave my A.A. friends. I would forget all I had learned. I would go out again and get hurt some more. Then I would come crawling back, asking for help.

People at A.A. were always willing to help me. But I did not want to help myself. Not 100 percent, anyway. I would use a part of the program. The rest, I would do my way. During this time, I hit quite a few hospitals. I did quite a few short stints in jail. But I also went to school. I got a good job in the medical field. But I didn't like to stay at one job for too long. I didn't want people to learn how much I drank.

During these dry spurts, I also would work in my

community. I had a high post with a political party. I was a delegate for a national union. But sooner or later, I would go out and blow it all by drinking. I did not feel I deserved anything good. I didn't know myself that well. And what I saw in myself, I didn't like. So I would go back to my bottle. Now the blackouts came more often. I once woke up in Miami Beach with a hangover and sunstroke. And I didn't even remember leaving New York.

I began to believe that I was nuts. I thought that's why A.A. wasn't working for me. The people in the program were nice. I wanted to be one of them. But I just could not be honest. I went on like this for eight years. There were a dozen more arrests. I received the last rites half a dozen times. I wrecked cars. I lost jobs. I had a marriage that lasted only three weeks.

Then I woke up standing before a judge again. I saw my whole life flash by. He sent me right back to an upstate prison. I was sent to Sing Sing. I would lie in my cell at night. I tried to figure out where I went wrong. After a couple of weeks there, I was sent to "Little Siberia." It was a prison far away from New York and my home.

This was the place where I learned about sobriety. I had a lot of time to get to know myself. I really thought that I wasn't a bad guy. In fact, when I didn't drink, I was a pretty nice guy.

I went to the A.A. meeting there. I was depressed. I saw about 10 guys telling jokes. They were having a good time. I talked to the group chairman. I asked him what was happening. He told me they didn't feel a part of A.A. They were in the joint. They couldn't drink anyway. I asked him if I could share with the guys.

That night when I spoke, A.A. had a different meaning to me. All of a sudden, the whole program made sense. It was like someone else was talking. It was another voice from deep inside of me. What came out surprised me. The guys must have liked what I had to say. At the next meeting, they elected me group chairman.

Because I got involved, a few of my friends in the joint gave it a shot, too. More and more inmates joined. We started a treasury. We elected a program chairman, a G.S.R. (general service representative), and a secretary. We continued to grow. Some A.A. friends from Canada came to help us in our meetings.

We began with 10 people meeting once a week. We grew to 70 people meeting twice a week. We got into Step meetings and the Traditions. A lot of outside A.A. people helped with literature and moral support. Our members began to know what it felt like to be a real part of something. Maybe for the first time in their lives. And it was something good and beautiful.

Last February, we had our first group anniversary. Some 200 people were there. The guys in the group really put a lot of work into it. I also celebrated my first sober anniversary on that day. I felt something I had never felt before. I can't explain it. I can only say it was electric. I was sober for one year. I could honestly say that I liked what I saw in myself.

For the first time in my life, I was grateful to be alive. I had the power to think and plan. I felt I knew what life is all about. I felt I could love and be loved. I never want to forget all the joy at that meeting. When things seem dark, I can always reach into my memory bank. I can gain strength from recalling that day.

I left the prison last month. Now I am in a work release program near home. I go to work five days a week. I go to A.A. at night. Each weekend, I go home and stay with my loved ones. I can care about the people that I love today. I get up in the morning and thank my Higher Power. I have a toll-free number to Him today. I can call and ask Him to help me. I can also say thanks.

I like being sober. I like being a part of A.A. I am grateful that I was given another shot at A.A. I know what being grateful means. I will always feel a part of that A.A. group in prison. It took the unselfish sharing of a bunch of cons to teach me. And I am grateful for that. I hope someday to go back there. To share with some others who might not be as lucky. I know that to stay sober, I have to share it. I can't think of a better way than this: to give it back to the people in our prisons. They played a very important part in my life.

Thanks, A.A. Thanks, God. And thanks to all the A.A.s in all our prisons.

—R.M., East Meadow, NY

FREEDOM

In the March [1959] Grapevine is an article called "A Good Gripe." It is by an inmate in the Massachusetts State Prison. His name is Ray. He asks the questions: Why is A.A. at prisons? People can't get drunk there?

I agree with Ray that inmates can get booze. But I wonder if, for an alcoholic, that isn't a problem besides alcohol. I believe there is a greater danger. It is the mental and emotional binge. It can happen anywhere, anytime. That's my experience. I wonder if there are others who feel the same way.

In '53 and '54, I served 17 months in a small western prison. There was no A.A. group. No treatment program of any sort. And not enough work. Less than 25 percent of the inmates were working. I decided I would take it easy. I would solve all of my problems on the day of my release. I settled down to do some fancy daydreaming.

Nothing bothered my daydreams. They were all about me… me… me…. It turned out to be 17 months of wasted time. I went 17 months in prison without a drink. But every day I was drunk on the wine of my fantasies.

On my release, the free world was a shock. It did not match my prison daydreams. Or care about my big ego. I started drinking. It took the rough edge off of reality. I had been back with my wife and two children for just four months. And I found myself before a judge again. Being tried for forgery again.

But that judge knew of my drinking. He knew about A.A. In spite of my record, he put me on probation. But he told me to attend A.A. meetings. I went to meetings for a year. I stayed sober during that time. I believe it was because of the fellowship I found in the A.A. group. I didn't have much use for those Twelve Steps. I thought they were for the "weak sisters."

I ended up going on only one more drunk…but it lasted six months. During the last few weeks of that binge, I went to the upper Midwest. I was on a "travel now—pay later" plan. The "pay later" part cost me 14 months in a Wisconsin prison.

At the prison, I began seeing a psychiatrist. I discovered how crazy my life had been. At the same time, I began finding meaning in our Sunday morning A.A. meetings. The A.A. and the therapy began waking me to reality.

But it was a difficult recovery. I fought it every step of the way. I kept looking for ways to keep from changing. In time, though, I came face to face with myself. I saw what a hell of a mess I had made of my life. It was hard to live with myself. I saw how rotten I had been. What a liar I had been. All the heartache I had caused. A growing sense of guilt finally broke me. One lonely night, I was in despair. I turned to God with the whole mess. I felt helpless and truly sorry. Maybe for the first time in my life.

I can remember asking for strength, mercy, and forgiveness. God performed His greatest miracle that night. He forgave me. He filled me with a strength I never knew before. I went to bed exhausted, and slept deeply.

That happened 15 months ago. I haven't known a bad

day since. The ghosts of the past are still with me: I'm still locked up. I am now serving time in a county jail in southern Minnesota. And the end is still not in sight. There are other charges I have to answer for.

But the pain has been removed. Contact with my Higher Power has been restored. A strange new peace and quiet stays with me. That odd hurt in my chest is gone. So is my nervous, restless fear.

It may sound crazy to feel freedom in jail or prison. But that's exactly what I have. I've known more freedom in these past 15 months than in all my 32 years of life. My doubts are gone. I counsel and perform A.A. service for my fellow inmates. Since I came out of my shell, they are like brothers to me. I see them struggle with the same problems that depressed me!

I'm content to leave my physical freedom in the hands of God. That fact alone is a miracle for me! People see the way I've changed. I have new friends working to help set me free. My sentence here is very small. It should have been much greater.

Finally, I heard from my wife. It was the first time in over a year. By a miracle of faith, she and the children are waiting for me. I know now what the Bible means when it says, "My cup runneth over...."

It would probably make a better A.A. story if I hadn't needed help. So many other people outside of A.A. have helped me change: therapy, religion, and support from many wonderful people at the Wisconsin State Prison. All had a hand in my journey from wet to dry.

In therapy, I learned many new truths. I got my inventory started. I found myself a beginner in the A.A. program. I had joined our prison A.A. group to impress the parole board. Now, I can no longer kid myself. And so the urge to impress other people is leaving me.

I still feel the danger of emotional binges. But now I see

them for what they are: the lead in to an actual drunk. I know of only one tool to guard against both the dry drunk and the wet drunk: Alcoholics Anonymous. I join Ray, and the thousands like us, who are grateful that A.A. is in the prisons.

I work to spread the good news about A.A. right here in the county jail. A court order permits me to attend an intergroup session. It will be held in this city. I'm going to speak to that group. If I tell them nothing else, they are going to hear this: how the quiet hand of God came into my life. And how I gave my life to Him when His truth made me free. That's God—as I understand Him.

–Merv K., New Ulm, Minnesota

NICE JEWISH GIRLS
DON'T GO TO PRISON

I grew up in a typical American household. My mom was the homemaker. My Dad went out to work. We celebrated all the Jewish holidays. I don't remember alcohol ever being a problem at our family parties. But I do remember my father drinking a lot. He kept his alcohol on a shelf above the telephone in the kitchen. That was off limits for us.

I had my first drunk at my brother's wedding. I was 14 years old. The wedding was at a fancy Jewish country club in Houston, Texas. I threw up on my dress. My mom was not happy with me. She sent me home.

When I turned 15, I met my first love. My parents used to let us drink at our house. We thought that was cool.

At 17, if you were a good Jewish girl, you went to Israel. When I was there, I found out my father had left my mother. (He'd left her the day he took me to the airport.) My cousin was on the trip with me. He held me as I cried. That night he took me out. We drank vodka and orange juice.

When I came home to Texas, my life had changed. My parents had divorced. My boyfriend was entering a pre-med program. His parents had told him that he'd be better off without me. He agreed. Three months later, my cousin shot himself in the head. It took me a long time to get over his death.

College came next. I didn't get good grades. So my father made me go to work. I went to work for a health center in Houston. I started taking diet pills. I also started writing my own prescriptions. I didn't get caught—that time.

When I was 26, I met the man of my dreams: a parcel delivery man. As it turned out, he delivered more than packages. He was a former drug user. Now he was an active drinker. He introduced me to martinis. I thought I had died and gone to paradise. I was hooked right away. From that moment on, we were tied together by vodka and foggy love.

We spent our first Fourth of July together. He was arrested for public drunkenness. I was sent home. I bailed him out of jail. I told him that I never wanted to see him again. We moved in together soon after that. His two-year-old daughter moved in with us. I took on the role of mommy.

We got married in the synagogue I had grown up in. I was badly hung over. We spent our honeymoon in the Napa Valley. It's a wine valley in California. It was a total drink fest. You could use the video of the trip in a drunk-driver's class: It shows how alcoholism progresses.

The following years were hard. I crossed that invisible line with my drinking. I also got pregnant. I did not want to drink when I was pregnant. But it was rough. So, I drank. I knew it was wrong, but I couldn't stop. I had no idea that I was an alcoholic. Why would I? I drank a gallon of milk each day. It helped to cancel out the alcohol. (Later, I read the Big Book story about the man who drank whiskey and washed it down with milk. That was just like me.)

On the Internet, I read how alcohol can hurt a baby in the womb. I read so much about it that I was almost an expert. But I still drank when I came home from work. The disease had a hold on me.

I even drank the morning my son was born. Lennie was born four weeks early. He suffered from weak lungs. We spent the next four weeks in the hospital unit for sick babies. My husband said, "If anything is wrong with him, I will never forgive you." I was filled with guilt. I could hardly stand it. I had to drink. I had to numb the pain in my heart.

I had to go home from the hospital without my baby. I was crushed. I sat beside his empty cradle every night and cried. I had not bonded with my son. I was so afraid I had hurt him for the rest of his life. Then the doctor told me that Lennie was fine. He had only been sick because he was born early. But I still had a hard time accepting that. My therapist begged me to tell the doctor about my drinking. But I couldn't. I was too scared.

Finally, I brought my baby home. That day, I cried so hard with joy that I could hardly see. I swore off liquor and thanked God. But that did not keep me sober.

The scary day came when I was taking a shower. The baby ran out the front door. He ran around the block by himself. I found him in the arms of the lady at the gas station. I was frightened and ashamed. I was also hung over.

When I got home, I phoned my sister-in-law. I told her what had happened. Two hours later, she and my brother were at my door. They took me to the hospital to get help for my drinking.

Once we got there, my sister-in-law told the doctors what had happened. Within five minutes, Child Protective Services arrived. I begged my brother to take me home. As I left, I vowed never to drink again. The next day, my husband put his foot down. He told me to check in to another hospital. If I didn't, he would divorce me. So I went. But less than four hours later, I checked myself out.

My mother was living across the bayou from us. She was suffering from a nerve disorder. She was drinking, and roaming the streets at night. She was admitted to the psych ward. It was the same one I had been in. Then I told my brother I needed help. I told him I was losing it. I was trying to hold myself together. I was trying to take care of my

mother, a new baby, and a little girl. All while I was drinking.
I also still had my job. Then my office had "Take Your
Daughter to Work Day." So I took my daughter to work. But I
was drunk. The next day, I checked into Spring Shadows Glen
for 28 days of treatment. I was told that I was an alcoholic.
I told them, "Not until I drank my hair spray. That's when I
knew something was very wrong with me."

After 28 days, I went home. Then I went on vacation,
and drank again. I could not get sober. I was confused and
depressed. I started to drink hair spray every day. I became
deathly sick. My husband took me to a women's center. But I
ran away the next day. I was out of my mind. I was run down
and beaten up from alcohol. But that did not stop me.
I drank again.

Then my A.A. angel appeared. She made a Twelve Step
call on me. She and another A.A. took me to a women's
center in Pasadena. This place was the real deal. It was filled
with straight-off-the-street women. It took my soul straight
away. That's the only way I can describe it. I kept telling my
husband, "I'm going to die here." That's how I truly felt. But
everyone kept telling him, "Leave her there."

Finally, I came back home. I was numb. My husband and
I went to an A.A. meeting that night. I got a sponsor. The next
day in my backyard, I felt the Spirit move through me. I fell
to my knees. I begged for help. I was truly sick and tired of
being sick and tired.

I started to sober up. I had lost weight after having the
baby. But it started coming back. So I began taking diet pills
and writing fake prescriptions.

Then one day it happened: I was arrested. Fortunately,
I did not have my son with me. I was taken to jail. I was
depressed and frightened. I thought I was going to prison.
Nice Jewish girls don't go to prison. Then my husband got
there around midnight. He was with my little girl. He got
me out.

I was facing a felony sentence. I was scared out of my mind. I started to drink again. I went to my pretrial hearing. And I was drunk. The judge was not there. I was sent home. I tried to detox myself. But I was having a rough time of it. I was shaking and throwing up. Again, my A.A. angel arrived. She told my husband to buy me a pint of whiskey. And then get me to the hospital to detox.

When we got there, I finally saw what was happening to me. I told God, "It's up to you now." But five days later, my son had an asthma attack. He needed medical attention. I left the detox. It was before my court date. I thought it would be okay: I was under a doctor's care.

It was not okay. My attorney said the judge would have me arrested. I had better check into treatment for another 28 days. But we had no insurance left. I began to panic. I begged my husband to put my treatment on his credit card. He did not like it. But I checked into a center that Thursday.

Unfortunately, the paperwork and the warrant got crossed. I was arrested the next day. My attorney promised to have me out that night. I ended up spending a week in the county jail.

But I was sober. I told myself that this was the end of my old life. I prayed and went to two A.A. meetings. At last, I knew what I had to do: stay sober.

When I was released, my brother took me back to treatment. The next day, my husband served me divorce papers. I was crushed. But I knew he wanted to stop the lies and the insanity. I went back to work. But I was "let go."

My job had ended. I was moving again. And I was getting divorced. But I was sober.

The judge was satisfied with my treatment. The court sentenced me to two years' probation and Prison for a Day. I was taken to a women's prison in Dayton, Texas. They put me in the scared-straight program. It did scare me—straight out of my mind. But I didn't drink. God had removed the obsession from me. I was following my sponsor's suggestions. And suggestions from everyone around me.

My home group became my safe haven. I was able to go back to work. I became school secretary at the synagogue. I had been blessed there as a small child. I had been honored there as a young teen, becoming an adult. And I had been married there. I guess God wanted me where he could keep an eye on me.

Here and in the rooms of A.A., I have started to put my life together. It has changed so much, I sometimes shake my head. I wonder, "What was that all about?" Now that we are divorced, my ex-husband and I are great friends. We go about life raising our children. I have also moved into a new apartment. It is small, but just right for me.

Once a month, I go to my probation officer. She still reminds me of the problems my alcoholism caused. The good news is that it's almost stress-free. I am sober. I go to at least four or five meetings a week. I have never been happier.

My meetings and my Step work are my first priorities— even over my son. Twice a month, I take a meeting to a women's center. It brings me back to where I used to be.

I have a sponsor. She has been there for me my entire sober time. To help me get sober, she made many Twelve-Step calls on me. Without her help, I wouldn't be here today.

I also met a gentleman with 17 years of sobriety. He taught me how to use the Steps in everyday life. He is a dedicated and grateful A.A. He has taught me to stay in reality. I have learned to look at things for what they really are, not for what I want them to be.

I use the Third Step every day of my life. I can turn my will and my life over to the care of God. That takes a lot of stress off me. You see, it's not up to me anymore. My sobriety is a gift from God.

—Sherri B., Houston, Texas

FROM THE INSIDE OUT

I was sentenced to 100 years in a maximum security prison. I was hopeless. I had no future. I was set to spend year after year watching life pass me by. I was supposed to have a career, a place in society. But my fear, resentment, and wrong actions always ruined me.

I tried to fill the hole in my soul. I used many things, including alcohol. It led to crime and jail. There was no way out for me. No reason for me to try any longer. At least, that's what I thought. Then I was brought to Alcoholics Anonymous in prison. And my life began to change from the inside out.

Right away, I felt the spirit of joy and fellowship in the rooms of A.A. For me, the meetings were a shelter from the lonely prison setting. I felt better in the meetings. That kept me coming back. I grew close to the outside sponsors who brought us meetings. I heard things that I believed. I wanted what the members had. So I took suggestions. I began to take on responsibilities within the group. The volunteers guided me. And I learned the value of service.

I worked with Jim, an A.A. volunteer who later became my sponsor. Outside, he had taken part in a Twelve Step workshop. He wanted to introduce the workshop in our prison. Because of A.A.'s track record—and with some help from our Higher Power—we were permitted to hold the workshop. It was the first of its kind in any prison. The warden even gave us several rooms to use. This let each inmate do a Fifth Step in private with an outside sponsor.

Seventeen inmates started the workshop. Five completed all Twelve Steps. Then they began to sponsor other inmates. We held three more workshops over the next three years. It showed that A.A.'s program of recovery can work anywhere.

In our second year, my sponsor went to the Maryland A.A. State Convention. When he came back, he said, "I want to bring a convention to the prison. I believe it will help any recovering alcoholic."

Hold a convention in a maximum security prison? At first, it seemed impossible to pull off. It took three years of planning. It took a lot of talking with the prison supervisors. But we formed a convention schedule. It fit with the security policies. It fit with the prison's daily schedule of activities. We finally received permission to hold an A.A. Prison Convention. But problems rose. A date was set four times during the year. For various reasons, the warden canceled each date.

The project's leaders—both civilians and inmates—became frustrated. They were ready to scrap the project. But then, on our fifth try, the warden approved the date. It was set for Friday and Saturday, August 17 and 18, 2001. We had local and regional A.A. speakers. We also had three inmates to speak. And we brought in a speaker from California. We held four workshops: Sponsorship, The Twelve Steps, Spiritual Experience, and Acceptance. Catered meals were served. Nearly 50 inmates, both male and female, were included. Over 35 outside guests took part. We even held a sobriety "countdown." A.A.s were counting from 17 years of sobriety all the way down to six hours!

Let me tell you, that prison convention may have been small. But the hope and spiritual power there could match any meeting. Any size. It had to be one of the highlights of my time in prison. It was a true gift of the program. A few months after the event, we started a new Twelve Step workshop. It had more inmates than ever before. Many came because of the prison convention.

I kept on helping others through A.A. Then a chance for release came my way. I had spent almost 11 years in prison. I had a far better life than I had ever known before. I had tried to live one day at a time. I had tried to live by spiritual principles. I had stayed close to the A.A. Fellowship. I had trusted God and my sponsor. They had carried me through my prison time.

Now, I had a second chance at freedom! I remember an A.A. speaker saying, "When God has work for you to do, the walls come down." My sponsor would say, "When the system shuts a door in your face, God opens a window." I had been turned down for parole nine times. I had learned to accept God's will. And I had known peace, even in prison.

On Good Friday, 2002, I was released. My sponsor was waiting for me in the parking lot. We had talked ahead of time. We had agreed: I should jump into the program as soon as my feet hit the sidewalk. I walked out of the prison. And 20 minutes later, I made my first stop in society at two A.A. clubhouses in the area. They were the Alano Club and the Serenity Center.

My sponsor drove me to the recovery house where I now live. That evening, I attended the ABC Group. It was my first A.A. meeting as a free man. Two days later, I celebrated Easter Sunday at my sponsor's house with his family. There were no happier or more grateful people in Maryland. My sponsor and I talked about our growth in the program, and how the Steps can change lives. Of how God gives hopeless people a second chance, so we can live a life beyond our dreams.

I had nearly 10 years of sobriety then. But my sponsor suggested I act like a newcomer. He said I was new to society. I trusted him and A.A. I followed the suggestions. I did 120 meetings in 90 days. I joined my sponsor's home group. I took a service position at the local intergroup. I tried to help others on a daily basis.

During this time, I attended four A.A. conventions and one spiritual retreat. My sponsor and I spoke of how wonderful it was to live one's dreams in a spiritual way. To be a source of love and kindness in the world, and to pass this program on to the newcomer. My two years in A.A. have taught me this: Sponsorship, the Steps, and Service are the core actions that keep me sober. Someday, I hope to carry the lessons of love and service back into a prison and give back what was passed on to me.

—J.K., Baltimore, MD

ON THE
JAILHOUSE FLOOR

Life has so many twists. You can't tell where it's going to take you. My journey began on Day One of my sobriety. I was fresh out of the Los Angeles County Jail. I walked from my parent's home into a brand new life.

When I came back to Alcoholics Anonymous, I was broke. Family, friends, or foes could not trust me. My mother had told me, "Nobody loves you but your mama. And she might be jiving too." She was old and tired. She did not want any more violence in her home. My father had said, "If you ever set foot on my property again, I'll kill my oldest son." He was talking about me.

I had been discharged from Camarillo State Hospital. It was the second time. The next day, I arrived drunk at my parents' home. In a blackout I beat my father. I hurt the only friend I had left in this world. He had stood in long lines at the county jails to see me. He had taken long bus rides to the state hospital. Just so his oldest son would have cigarette money.

My family had me arrested. When I got out of jail the next day, I went back to their home. I was drunker and crazier than the previous day. I saw my aunt crossing the street. That wine told me to get her, too. I chased her into her home. But she was not running from her nephew. She was running to get the pearl-handled .38 pistol. She kept it in her bedroom. I saw her come out with that pistol. I knew she would pull the trigger. I ran behind her home. I jumped over the fence. I ran down the alley. I found a large trash can. And I hid inside for a very long time.

My family had me arrested for the second time. I sat on that cold jailhouse floor. And there I had my first spiritual awakening. I thought about all the people who had tried to help me. They tried to get me off alcohol. I saw how I had turned up my young nose at them. I saw for the first time: If I was going to recover, I would have to work at it.

I served my one day in the county jail. I had wanted to go back to Alcoholics Anonymous. But I made one mistake: I had slept by the toilet. Everybody in that jail cell "let go" on me. That next morning in court, I was a sight to be seen.

After I was released from jail, I broke into my father's home. I was taking my brother's clothes. My mother walked in on me. I said bad things to her. I turned to walk away. Then I heard my mother say, "I want you to know, son, that mama loves you. But you are an alcoholic. There's nothing mama can do about that."

I had no place to go that night. I had my one day of sobriety. Then I remembered the only place that might welcome me back. I walked to the Friday night beginners' group at South Figueroa Street.

God placed a sober member of Alcoholics Anonymous in my life that night. This A.A. member was struggling with his sobriety. But he was practicing the Twelfth Step. He knew that work with another alcoholic would help him too. I listened to him share his experience, strength, and hope. He was sad and hurt: He could not see his two daughters. After the meeting, I let him give me a ride. But I was too proud to tell him the truth. I had no place to go. No place to lay my head that night. I told him to pull over at the next corner. I said I'd walk the rest of the way home.

The only homes I knew were old parked cars, doorways, and crawl spaces. I hung my head and began walking. I walked toward skid row. I would sleep in the all-night movie theater. My God whispered to me in that quiet voice. He said, "If you go back to skid row, you go to die. You won't come back this time."

I turned around and walked to my father's home. I knocked on the door. I asked my father to please help me. Help me one more time. This time I thought I could stop drinking. Do I have the kind of love for my children that my father had for me? The kind of forgiveness? I don't know. I can only hope I do. I hope this spiritual program of action will lead me there.

I have had more spiritual awakenings since my first day sober. As I look back, one stands out. It was a turning point of my sobriety. I got to share at the Friday night beginners' group. It was my first time speaking there. I ended my sharing with: "One day my ship's going to come in. And everything's going to be all right. Keep coming back, newcomer. The program works."

I really thought I had shared something wise. Then the group leader called on this woman. She had long-term sobriety. She shared from her heart with love and compassion. She said, "If your ship's tied up in harbor, life might smash it against the rocks. You might want to put your ship in God's hands. Because faith without works is dead."

For the past 29 years, I have been putting my faith in God. I have worked to do God's will. I have given my God the credit for all my work. Without my God, I am truly nothing.

I came back to Alcoholics Anonymous truly hopeless. Now, I have become the first member of my family to get a master's degree. My therapist said I was a drunk who could never live in society. He said I could only live in a board-and-care home. Or in some mental institution and only on medication. But I am a free human being today. I have placed my life in the hands of a Power—a Power much greater than myself.

I would like to thank the members of Alcoholics Anonymous. They have been the shining lights. They have guided me to this higher plane of living. May peace, love and hope be with you. Every day of your lives.

—Jerome R.S., Corona, California

MIRACLES HAPPEN

I grew up as a military brat. We moved every two years. So I have been familiar with "geographical cures." I've had to change friends. I've had to make new ones. I was always trying to fit in.

About age 12, I was hanging around a group of 16 year olds. They introduced me to a whole new life—a life of booze and drugs. I started just for fun. Then I began drinking at the bus stop before school. It didn't take long. That mental obsession captured my mind and spirit. It took away my choices. It led me down many a dark path. I experienced blackouts and vomiting. I had bad relationships. I got pregnant at age 16. And thoughts of suicide followed.

I would love to tell you that I got pregnant and stopped drinking. But I couldn't quit. I am not proud of that fact. But it is the cold, hard truth.

I was married and divorced. I had other relationships. I was living life hard and fast. I was proud of myself. I never had been in trouble with the law. Many of my friends had been to jails or treatment centers. I had been told a lot of times: "You can't control your drinking." But I didn't think I had a problem.

Then I got arrested. I felt such guilt, shame, and regret. My sister called me. We argued. We said some hurtful, awful things. I told her I wouldn't speak to her again. For the next five years, we stayed away from each other. We lived in the same town, but didn't speak. The resentment was like a fire burning in my soul.

I lived in constant fear of police, of attorneys, of friends, of financial insecurity, of everything. How could this be happening to a nice young lady like me? I was in denial: I was guilty of the charges.

While I was in jail, I attended my first A.A. meeting. They read the Steps and the Traditions. But they didn't apply to me. They could have been a foreign language for all I knew. A blind man told his story. He talked about his alcoholism. How he had cabdrivers help him get his booze. Now he lives without booze.

On Thursdays, they would put us in a white van. They'd take us to a treatment center for a Twelve Step meeting. It was where some of my friends had gone. A guy who spoke sounded like Lawrence Welk. He talked of how he was addicted to cough syrup. I thought, "If I ever get that bad, I would quit too."

No one told me that I should go to A.A. meetings when I got out. So, I didn't. The next 12 years got worse for me. I got to understand insanity.

That hole in my soul got bigger. I had felt it most of my life. I felt it through all the years that I drank. Then I finally had a clear moment. I faced new fears. I said out loud, "Do you think that I need help?"

I felt all kinds of fear: Fear of change. Fear of the unknown. Fear of failure. But none of these were as great as this fear: continuing to live in hell. My hell was made up of mental twists and of the obsession for alcohol. I felt out of control, and worthless.

I asked for God's help. I walked into an A.A. meeting. I

was scared, crying and shaking. After several weeks, I heard another alcoholic say it: She talked about the hole in your soul where the cold wind blows. But now it is filled in the shape of God. I understood that. There was an idea that I could hold on to. Today my life is so full. It has come from taking the Twelve Steps. And I've tried to live by spiritual principles.

While I was in prison, my parents and my son would visit me. It was 100 miles one way. My mom is not an alcoholic. But she went to an A.A. meeting with me. I still remember it with love. It was as though God had everything planned. There were two seats up front, and my mom and I sat there. The ladies brought up the topic of moms. Some were moms. Some had moms who drank and used. So everyone shared an experience.

The second lady shared. Then my mom got up. She asked who it was that spoke. Then she went over and hugged the lady. We all started crying. It was a very touching and spiritual meeting. I didn't ask my mom. I just suddenly said, "Tonight everyone has a mom." And she hugged everyone as they left the room. There wasn't a dry eye in the house.

Today life is so different. I have gone from hopeless to hopeful. I've carried a meeting into a local jail for the last 3½ years. We started in a small room the size of a walk-in closet. We sat on the floor on our Big Books. Now, we are helping form policies for the new jail.

God has blessed us. We have groups who contribute funds for Big Books. One was a women's group: Each member signed a book so the reader would receive love and prayers. Also, our clubhouse took collections in a coffee can. The can had a label that said, "Big Bucks for Big Books."

A lady I used to sponsor attended a few of our jail meetings. Then she stopped coming. She used to say, "I know what I need to do. When I get out, I need to call and go to A.A." The hand of God was still there. When she got out, she was offered a ride. But she chose to get into another car with a lady released that day. They drank and used. Eight hours later, she was killed in an auto accident. I didn't want her death to be in vain. I asked the ladies to write something in her honor. The article was called, "So You Think You Are Different." It was published in our state prison newsletter, Bars and Cells.

I knew that I wanted to work in corrections. So I got involved with our state Correctional Facilities Committee. I became treasurer. Someone in the program gave us a used computer. We then got a reduced price on Third Edition Big Books. It was amazing.

The miracle of sobriety happens for thousands of recovering drunks like me. We share our experience with each other, and with ex-inmates. I have the privilege of writing a lady who attended our meetings. She is 25 years old, and doing a life sentence. We talk about miracles, prayers, and God. I talked about breaking my anonymity to my employer. That allowed me to change shifts, so I can attend correctional events. Our committee glows with love, laughter, and sharing the gift of recovery. It's funny: We used to run from the law and jails. Now we can't wait to get into them. Today some committee members wear striped uniforms to A.A. events. It helps people see that we need funds for literature.

Here are some other miracles: There is the love in A.A. and the people that God puts in your life. One friend is helping me to get back my right to vote. When I was younger, it didn't matter. Then when they took the right to vote away, it still didn't matter. But today I'm a member of society. I want to stand and be counted. Remember that sister that I didn't speak to? She called me several years ago. She said she needed help. Today she is trying this way of life, one day at a time. And we love each other.

I couldn't have imagined all of these miracles. God has

given them to me, and so many others in recovery. I was able to visit that same son in Anchorage, Alaska. I went to an A.A. meeting with him. My grandkids have never seen me drunk. God willing, they never will.

I believe so much in miracles that my license plate says, "MIRACLES HAPPEN." Another says, "A MIRACLE." I love attending meetings with the ladies who heard the message behind the walls. They are now in A.A., not just around it. If these miracles can happen for me, they can happen for you. So, let the miracles happen!

—Mandy S., Nashville, TN

SAVED FROM HERSELF

"I'm broken." I moaned those words quietly. I was clinging to the bars of the cellblock. I was too weak even to weep. A voice came from the other side: "That's good; it's exactly where you need to be." I was shocked. I tried to figure out that simple truth. But my mind was still fogged by my latest blackout drunk. The chaplain spoke gently to my heart. He explained that I first must be brought to my knees. Then he offered words of hope. He said, "Your humiliation can be turned into humility." He called humility "the basic ingredient in any recipe for recovery."

I was confused. You see, at 13 years old, I had put up with my father's beatings. They broke my spirit. He called them "spankings." After that I made a silent vow: I would never again let anyone "break" me. No one would ever beat me into surrender. So how, 35 years later, did I find myself here? Why was I feeling so broken? Why did the thought of surrender seem so pleasing? Surrender to anything that might ease my pain? And what about my vow? The questions were cunning, baffling and powerful. Just like my disease.

One thing was certain: I was ready "to be willing to be

willing." I wanted to get honest. I thought about my 20 years of hanging around Alcoholics Anonymous. Hadn't I tried that easier, softer way? Hadn't it failed me? But here I was, locked up. Life, as I knew it, was over. My reality now included two felony charges. So it seemed wise to listen to the chaplain. And listen to the A.A. people. I'd better pray that I could hear their message. After all, what did I have to lose? And so, I did listen, and listen, and listen. And soon, I began to hear.

Long ago, I had admitted that I was alcoholic. I even admitted that I was powerless over the drug. But in my sick mind, that fact was a badge of honor. I could not admit that my life had become unmanageable. As the fog slowly lifted from my mind, I heard a message: "If I only work Step One halfway, I might as well not work it at all." Step One is the only Step that we can, and must, work perfectly. I hadn't planned to be in jail. So, maybe my life was becoming unmanageable.

The months passed. I struggled to stay open-minded. I began to hear other messages. "More will be revealed," they said. And how right they were!

I began to get honest about what had brought me to this bottom: my own self-will run riot. I also began having clear moments. I suddenly saw that I had been true to my vow. I hadn't let anyone else break me. I had protected myself from others. I had hurt myself. My Higher Power, who is God, had let me break my own spirit! God does, indeed, work in strange ways.

I would learn many lessons in A.A. I learned that I had surrendered to alcohol from the age of 16. I was held hostage by a power greater than myself. Since I am truly powerless, why not give up the power of alcohol? Open up to the Power of God! I learned that no program of recovery will work for me. I must work for it. I learned that A.A. is a simple program. But it is not an easy one. Still, death of the mind, body and soul is a grim option.

This newfound knowledge was powerful. It let me see the answer to all of my problems: I must work to change myself. I cannot change others. Today, I work, 24 hours at a time. I work to turn my will over to the will of God. I pray daily, asking to know God's will. I am not a religious person. I don't like ritual. But A.A.'s spiritual principles continue to save my life—one day at a time. It is a pleasure to be alive today. And to help carry the message of Alcoholics Anonymous to those who still suffer. I'm very grateful. I had just enough sense left. The sense to let Alcoholics Anonymous and my Higher Power save me from myself!

—Paula O., Spring, Texas

HOW TO MAKE IT ON THE STREET

I was working to leave the state pen once I got there. I had a one-and-a-half-to-three-year term. I was on federal parole when I was sentenced. So I still owed the federal government five more years. I wasn't worried about living in prison. But, in the next one to seven years, I was going to be let out. I did not know how to live on the street.

I couldn't figure out what was wrong with me. Doctors had said I was crazy. I had hidden my alcoholism behind heavy drama.

I had a visit from some inmate A.A. members. I joined the Twelve Step Study School. For five weeks, they carried me through the Steps in the book *Alcoholics Anonymous*. In the sixth week, they let me go to the regular A.A. meeting on Friday night. It was a call-up speaker meeting. Real people from the outside could attend. With the help of my sponsor, I was given a new A.A. job: I took the next group through the Steps. We met at the Twelve Step Study School on weekends. I was lucky. I learned that life is not about what I can get. It's about what I can give. It is not about what God can do for me. It's about what God can do through me. I must be open to

69

life and to the Spirit.

Over the next 13 months, I continued to work with others. I learned how to do daily tasks. My job was in the dishroom. Although I didn't want to, I became the lead man there. I found a skill that has carried me throughout my life: I am able to get people to work together. I learned to serve as a leader. I was being prepared for life in the real world. That's where you show up and do what you agreed to do. That is the order of the day.

My sponsor, Bruce, was clear: Want money? Get a job. Show up for the job, on time, all the time. While you are there, do some work. At the end of the day, they will give you money. It will never be enough, but it will always be enough. When they ask you to do more, do it. As long as you take their money, be loyal. Keep your word. If you don't think you can keep your word, don't give it. Bruce gave me these principles. They guide my actions and my thinking.

I was granted parole to the federal authorities. We all thought that I would have to finish the federal sentence. A.A. people had shown me that I could be useful anywhere. So I got ready to return to federal custody. There was another possibility: The federal judge might parole me. My sponsor told me that he did not think I was ready to return to the street. But he said I should be ready. I spent the next three weeks studying my life. I looked at my intentions. I reworked the Steps. That way, I made sure I was not holding on to any old ideas. The kind of ideas that got me into trouble. I needed to be open. I wanted to be free to accept whatever happened. I wanted to be open to the guiding of the Spirit. When they took me to Denver for the federal hearing, I was ready.

The federal parole officer had once wanted to lock me up. He had said I could not be helped. Now he suggested that the federal judge parole me. He said that I had been going to A.A. He told me they would know within six days if I would make it or not. It was the Thursday before Memorial Day weekend, 1969. I got a federal parole. It was a long weekend because of the holiday. I had no job and no place to live. I had only $17 of my $25 release money. The parole officer and I agreed: It would be best if I stayed in jail until the new week started.

During the weekend, I set my mind to complete my parole. I wanted to live on as a free man. I had been told to go to A.A. my first day out. That way, I would probably stay out. I needed to remember that I was still doing time. I just was doing it on the street. I was not an ex-con. I was a man who had been to prison. Ex-cons have problems with the law and society. I was to let the Spirit guide me. To go where it led me. As long as it helped me stay out. The relationship I had formed with my Creator was on easy terms. Terms that worked. I could ask for direction and strength to do the right thing. And I would be given direction and strength.

Monday arrived. I walked down the row to meet the parole officer. Another inmate stopped me and gave me a slip of paper. He said, "If you have a problem getting a job, go see this guy. He can help." The federal people spoke with me. Then I was taken to the state parole officer. He was clear in his orders: "Have a job by tomorrow, or back you go. Report every evening after work."

I knew I could get a job at a hamburger joint in Aurora. I had worked there before. The manager was a good man. Despite my trouble, he would help. I went to catch the bus to Aurora. I hit my first hurdle. The sign on the bus said: HAVE EXACT FARE. DRIVERS CARRY NO CHANGE. I felt like I was falling apart. I could not get on the bus.

I remembered the slip of paper the inmate had given me. It was a daily labor pool. It was located only four or five blocks away. I walked to the labor pool. I had been told to be completely open and honest. Jack asked me what I wanted. I said, "My name is Don P. I am an alcoholic and have had drug problems. I am on federal and state parole. And I need a job. Do you have anything?"

Jack got excited. He said, "You are just what I have been looking for." He took me to a paper company. They told us that they did not hire ex-cons. But I could work on Jack's payroll. Then they would put me to work unloading boxcars. Jack got me work for the rest of the day. He helped me get work clothes. He helped me find a place to stay. I reported to the parole officer at the end of the workday. Then I followed directions. I went to the York Street Club to get with A.A.

While I was in prison, I had talked with a regular from the outside. His name was Reed. He had become a mentor for me. We were men who would normally not mix. He was an older man with class. He was a financial specialist, and a family man. He was always at the meeting when he said he would be. He had a two-hour drive each way. But he always showed up. He had qualities I wanted for myself. Just prior to release, I asked Reed, "How will I be accepted out there?" He said, "Well, you will just have to come and find out. Come to York Street your first night out. One of us will be there to meet you."

I was very nervous. I walked up the steps at York Street and went inside. There stood Reed. I had seen him once a month for over a year. But I still felt like a nobody. I said, "You probably don't remember me. But you told me to come here my first night out of prison." Reed laughed. We began a friendship that lasted until he died. His wife Dotty later told me about my first day at York Street. She said Reed made sure they got there early. Just to meet me. I often met Reed and Dottie at the top of the stairs. They taught me to be there when someone needed help.

I became a member of the Denver Young People's Group. An old-timer there also had served time. He told me to give myself entirely to A.A. for a year. Then I would never have to go back to prison, except on my terms. For the next six months, I was not allowed to have a car. The A.A. people made a deal: If I got to the meeting, someone would get me home.

There were many former inmates in A.A. My parole agreement did not allow me to associate with former inmates. I asked my parole officer about this. He said, "If it's for A.A. purposes, you had better hang out with them."

Our group sponsored two meetings a week. There was a Tuesday discussion, and a Sunday call-up speaker meeting. We also went to other meetings in the area. We wanted to be part of A.A. as a whole. We got involved in Twelfth-Step work: We talked at local schools and service clubs.

If I admired a quality in a person, I climbed into his hip pocket. I learned how he got that quality. And I tried to practice it. I picked my street sponsor because he was a family man. He was also our group's G.S.R. He was dedicated to A.A. I followed him around. I learned my main responsibility: To stay sober and help others get sober. I also had a responsibility to the past. And a duty to the future. My duty is to serve the Fellowship. To make sure that the person in A.A. 50 years from now gets what I got: the same chance to learn. And to live a life that makes sense.

For the next two years, everything I did—except for work—was with A.A. I was released from parole one and a half years early. I had started to learn to practice the A.A. principles in all of my affairs. My sponsor suggested that I take on more projects. Then he added, "Just don't have more affairs than you have principles."

Social Services gave me an order: Never try to impress them just to get my children back. I was to put my life in order, and they would watch. If they ever thought I would be a decent father, they would contact me. They returned my children after two and a half years. I was working as a truck driver for the paper company during the day. At night, I helped out in a house where drunks tried to get sober.

I've worked to clean up my past. It has been very important and rewarding work. It is second only to my work with other alcoholics. I held a job long enough to qualify for Social Security. The last nine years, I have worked in corrections. I've been with the Department of Corrections in North Carolina. I've also worked for community corrections in Colorado. We simply found ways to get the A.A. message into prisons.

I have been married to the same wonderful woman for 26 years. We do not fight. At home, our bathroom is larger than the cell I had in prison. My children are not afraid of me. My neighbors respect me. They teach me how to be a good neighbor. My children are having children. One of my grandsons has just given us a great-grandchild.

A.A. has allowed me to serve the Fellowship in important ways. How did I prepare for this? I learned to trust in God, clean house, and help others. I have joined in the fellowship of the Spirit. I have found a way of life better than any I could have dreamed of.

–Don P., Aurora, Colorado

FREEDOM IS
A STATE OF MIND

I had been invited back to the penitentiary. I had spent over two and a half years of my life there. This happened over a year after they had let me out. It was the anniversary of the treatment center there. I attended it while in prison. It was the second time that former inmates could return. They wanted us to share our experience with those who were still there. I was a little nervous walking in that gate. But I wouldn't have missed it for anything in the world. I am very thankful for my time there. I truly have a new life as a result.

The trip back brought a flood of memories: It was September of 1990. I had been sentenced to prison. I took that long bus ride to Lexington, Kentucky. Then I took the cab ride up to the federal penitentiary. During that trip, my mind was going 90 miles an hour: "You could run." "You must be crazy turning yourself in for three years flat." "What about your kids?" "It's too late to think about that now." "You did the crime. Now you must do the time." I couldn't seem to shut my head up. Not until the cab made its last turn: up the long, winding road to the penitentiary.

Then, it was like my whole body shut down and went

numb. I couldn't even remember getting out of the cab. Or going in gate after gate. I barely remember getting my bedding, uniforms, underwear, towel and washcloth. I was told to strip. Then take a shower. They covered my hair and body with a delouse spray.

On my return as a free woman, the anxiety came back. Much like that first day. But this time I could leave. I had to keep reminding myself of this. We were asked not to talk to friends we had left behind. We walked in silence through the main courtyard. Security thing, I guess. But there were six of us walking through that courtyard. We knew that was a huge symbol of hope.

My first room had 14 double bunk beds. It held 28 inmates. I knew a lot of people from the pen while I was out on the streets. They all told me, "You need to go in there. Mind your own business and do your time." This frame of mind kept me out of trouble. It's funny. You play cat-and-mouse with the police. And all that time, you accept that you'll go to jail. That the pen is one of the tough breaks of life. Much like someone that loses a job in the straight world. I knew this deep down: I didn't want to be the same as my friends. I didn't want to go in and out every six months. But I did not learn from their experience.

Today I shared a new experience. I shared how it is to live a life of recovery. I had only a year and a half sober. In that first year, I had a cop shake my hand. He told me what a good job I was doing. Now that was a new experience. In the past, the police only wanted my hand so they could put on the cuffs. This gave the girls a good laugh as I shared.

As an inmate, I was moved into a room that held four. I was given the job of orderly. That job is far from what you see in the movies. You work hard (at least I did). You get very little thanks. In fact, the other inmates can give you a pretty hard time. They would throw trash on the floor. They would put toothpaste on the mirrors. All because they would see you coming to clean. Lots of bathrooms to clean. Trash to collect. Floors to mop, then buff. I put everything I had into my work. It kept me from thinking. Your big reward was $5 a month.

I talked about my work in a convenience store making $6.50 an hour. I told them I was entering college. I spoke of goals I have today. Goals I would never have dreamed of a few years before. I told them the work was much the same. But the rewards were different. In that convenience store, I laughed. And I tried to make others laugh. I did very little laughing during the last years of my alcoholism.

I had started attending A.A. meetings. It was when I was on the street, waiting to be sentenced. I knew that I needed to keep going to meetings, even though I was locked up. They had two meetings a week in the main building. They were on Tuesday and Thursday nights. So, every Tuesday and Thursday I would go. Our compound held 2,000 women. There would be only 15-20 people at those meetings. Four or five of those people would be from an A.A. group on the outside. One day, I came back from a meeting. One of my roommates asked me, "Where do you take off to every Tuesday and Thursday night?" I answered, "Why?" She said, "Because when you come back, you seem at peace." She helped me see how important meetings are. I need them even when there isn't a threat of drinking and using.

During this weekend, I would receive my four-year sobriety coin. Bruin gave me my coin. He was an A.A. member from the outside. He had been there every Tuesday and Thursday of my two and a half years in prison. He shared, "The next person is an example of people that go to any length for their recovery. Tara came all the way from Washington State to celebrate her four years with us here in Kentucky." I was embarrassed. But I was also very proud as I received that coin. I still attend weekly meetings. I still get that peace of mind I found while I was locked up.

They put on a program to entertain us. They enacted a

play that brought back many memories. Then they sang "You Are My Hero." I never dreamed that someone would call me a hero. Tears rolled down my face. I remembered what made this wonderful weekend possible: It was the grace from God and my willingness.

I was always suspicious of prisoners who get religion. But there was something that happened when I lost everything. I don't mean my worldly possessions or my children. I'm talking about my dignity. My self-respect and hopes for life. I became open to the idea that I couldn't lose if I tried to believe in God.

I was born a Roman Catholic. I was raised in a Catholic school. As a child, I truly believed. But I began to doubt. It was because of bad behavior by people who acted like they were religious. I made a commitment to myself: I would never be one of those hypocrites. When I got into alcohol and drugs, I quit praying and believing. As an inmate, I was sitting behind walls and barbed wire fences. What did I have to lose? Now that I'm free, I just see myself as a Christian. I have a relationship with that Higher Power.

I remember the first time I trusted in my faith: They had a pilot one-year treatment program on the grounds. One of the counselors had encouraged me to go. I said I'd have to think about it. I might want to wait until I got closer to getting out.

I was wondering if I should go to treatment. I prayed and left it in God's hands. The very next day I was on the call out. Then the warden took me off. This happened three days in a row. Every night I would pray, "God, I am not going to make this decision. You know what bad decisions I make. Please guide me to do your will." On the fourth day, I went to the treatment unit.

The second day of my visit to the prison, I got to visit the treatment unit. It is separate from the rest of the compound. It is in a building of its own. As we walked that long road,

I recalled the first time I met Elaine: Shortly after I had arrived at the unit, she stood at my door. She was wringing her hands while she talked. She was about 10 years older than me. She was just about as nervous. But she didn't hide it as well as I did. "Hi, I'm Elaine," she said as she held out her hand, "You want to join me for dinner? I don't like crowds. So meet me right at the door. We can get ahead of the crowd when the bell rings."

Even being "ahead of the crowd" meant we were still in line. If we were 20-25 people from the front, we were doing well. I guess that is where I learned patience and tolerance.

Elaine and I became extremely close by standing in those lines, and by talking as we ate. We would meet each other three times a day. We began sharing small talk. As we learned to trust each other, we would share very private things.

In the drug treatment unit, we would go to class half a day. Then we worked the rest of the day. We had a Twelve Step meeting at night. We had all kinds of classes. We studied emotional responses. We studied criminal thinking. You name it, we had groups on it. We were also expected to do the Steps. We kept a daily journal. We handed it in to our counselors every day.

My second counselor, Cynthia, was no longer working there. But she had come back for the anniversary. She told me why she was there: because she heard I was coming back. She was always good for my self-esteem. She kept me as a client even after I graduated from the program. I only got a few minutes with her. Then we were rushed off to tour the building.

The building and the staff were almost the same. We visitors sat with the director, Dr. Simpson. A few staff members sat with us. We discussed our progress since our release. Sitting in that circle brought back my fear of authority. Or was it the powerlessness I had felt? And the willingness to learn? In my disease, I had always fought authority. I had lied and controlled every chance I got. I finally surrendered. But fear of myself came back. I became shy and boring. Now I sat in that circle again with the staff. I began feeling the same. I had to remind myself that we were all just people. We no longer had that teacher-student relationship.

As I sat in the circle, I kept thinking about my first counselor, Tonya. I was sad that she didn't come to the anniversary. Dr. S. told me that she called and sent her best. I'll never forget how much she helped me.

Her questions made me think. She read every journal entry. She would comment on each one. This was so important to me. My trust level was really low. When I would go to see her, we would sit and look at each other. She would ask me how I felt. I would say fine. It was like pulling teeth. But in my journal, I would tell her everything.

I remember walking into her office one time. I had just gotten word that my kids were in trouble. I thought, "I'm in the penitentiary. I'm helpless to do anything." Tonya encouraged me to brainstorm for solutions. She said, "What about their dad?" "He's in the penitentiary too. A lot of good he could do!" "What will it hurt to try? I can call his counselor and arrange a phone call." "Okay, but I don't see how he could help."

Thank God, I was wrong. He called his parents in Washington State. He hadn't talked to them in 10 years. They agreed to drive to Kansas City, Missouri. They picked up all three of our children. Then they brought them up in Auburn, Washington. My children's Aunt Nancy also helped. If I didn't believe in miracles before then, I did after that. Those events could not have happened without a miracle. That's why I ended up in Washington State. It's a trip I would have never planned to take. But now I'm glad I'm here.

Tonya also helped me see the shame and guilt I felt. It was over the loss of my hand. I sat in her office one day. She asked me about it. I sat there and lied. I said I grew up around a lot of handicapped people. Not having a hand didn't stop me. I always could do things you wouldn't believe. It never affected me. Her reply to me was, "If it didn't affect you, then why do you keep your arm in your pocket?" I didn't speak the rest of the session. But I wrote about it in my journal. I saw my shame and guilt over losing my hand. And I saw how drinking and drugs let me hide how I felt.

Today I don't carry the shame about my hand. Or my disease. I rarely notice people staring. I have accepted myself for who I am—with all my defects. Those who are uncomfortable have the problem, not me. It is really funny watching the parents of curious children. The children ask to look at my arm, or touch it. The parents get embarrassed. At times they try to stop their children. I always tell them it's all right. It's good for them to be curious. When children see that it doesn't hurt anymore, they are usually okay with it, too.

I thought about all the classes I had there. I believe that the real turning point for me was when I did the Fifth Step. That's when you share your moral inventory—what you did wrong. You share it with God, and with another person there. Elaine was my sponsor. We picked one of the classrooms away from everybody. I did my Fifth Step with her. I told her all the gory details of my life. I didn't understand how that would help. Now I do. It helps keep me from going back out and doing the same things again. Since then I've heard this saying: "You never know yourself until you have shared yourself with another." I believe that this saying explains my experience.

During my Fifth Step, Elaine shared her similar experiences. My eyes were opened to a whole side of my story. I had been blinded by my feelings of shame and guilt. They had warped my beliefs. Those beliefs kept me safe as a child. But they distorted my view of the world as an adult.

My feeling of freedom didn't come right away. It was a day

or two later. I realized that I didn't worry about what others thought. I could laugh and have fun no matter where I was. My spirit was free, even though my body was locked up.

As I walked down the halls past my old room, a smile came to my face. I think I smiled the rest of the weekend. I had left there with just about every strike against me: I was a woman and an alcoholic. I was handicapped. I was an ex-felon and a single mother of three children. And I was moving to a state where I didn't know a soul. I didn't even know the way around the block. Despite all this, I was making it. I felt more confident than I had ever felt in my life. I have a Higher Power that goes everywhere with me. I am free.

I still remember the first time I felt that way: I was sitting in the middle of my steel-framed bunk bed. I started to smile. I realized that freedom is just a state of mind. My bed was against two walls. I had only two and a half feet of space on either side. A door was at one end of the bed. A small window was at the other. A light from the hallway shined in the little window of the door. Outside there were fences, walls and doors. They kept me from physically leaving. But mentally, I was freer than I had ever felt in my life.

Today, I can share that special weekend. I can talk about the life that was behind it. I hope that others understand about their fight for freedom. It is an inward struggle. Freedom is a state of mind.

—Tara W.

BETWEEN THE LINES

There I was, locked up safe and sound. I thumbed through an issue of the Grapevine. The issue was dedicated to A.A. in prison. I came across a notice about the A.A. Corrections Correspondence Service. I thought about it for a minute, then moved on.

By the way, my name is Marty and I'm an alcoholic. I'm also in Colorado's Department of Corrections. I'm doing six sentences totaling 135 years. That's not a typo; it is 135 years.

A.A. in prison is nothing new to me. I was 17 years old when I was first introduced to A.A. I was doing time in a California prison. Even at that early age, I could relate to those who came in to sponsor our meetings. Deep in my heart, I knew that I had the disease of alcoholism. It ran in my family. I had a history of alcohol and drug abuse, but I had no desire to quit drinking.

By the age of 24, I was a divorced father of two. I was a drug abuser and a drunk. I was also on my way back to prison. I spent several weeks locked in a cell with nothing to do. I was allowed two books per week. They also let me have two or three hours of recreation in the gym. I spent many hours alone, bored and angry. One day, the alcoholism counselor, Pete, suddenly called me out of my cell.

Pete took me into his office. It was small and cramped. He had a heart-to-heart chat with me. Pete had a special approach. I didn't threaten him. He was not threatening to me. He didn't talk down to me. Prison officials usually do talk down to inmates. Instead, Pete sat his heavy frame down at his desk. He put his feet up. He asked how I was doing. He had a genuine concern for my welfare. He didn't want something from me. He wanted to be helpful. I told him I was bored from being locked up. I was waiting to be given a job and moved to another cell. He asked how long I would be there. I told him I'd be out in about six months. He asked what I was going to do when I got out. I told him I would go back to the town where I came from. I would sit in the local sports bar. I would drink shots of whiskey and ice-cold, longneck beer. I would get drunk. I'd pinch Tillie, my favorite bartender, every time she walked by.

Pete said, "Well, you're being honest." I told him I'd spent hours and hours pacing my cell. I'd been planning my next drunk, and counting the days. I just couldn't wait to get out and wrap my fingers around a cold, frosty beer. Pete told me that I was "dry, and thinking about drinking." Then I was sent back to my cell. I spent the next few days thinking about being "dry, and thinking about drinking." I couldn't argue with that. It was true.

As it turned out, Pete was just like me. He was new to the prison. And I was his first client. He was setting up treatment and education programs. When he introduced A.A. meetings, he invited me to go. I was all too happy to get out of that cell. I set up the room, made coffee, and sat in all the meetings I could. I cleaned up after the meetings. I also volunteered to do typing, and anything else that would get me out of that cell.

Before long we had five meetings per week. We had

speakers from the street. We had two Big Book studies every week. Many inmates couldn't read. So I got to read and reread a lot of the A.A. texts. It was Pete who gave me my first Big Book. He gave me my first "Twelve and Twelve," and more. I heard Pete's lectures so many times, I could teach them myself.

My plan for leaving in six months quickly changed. They added another year to my sentence. This took some of the wind out of my sails. It made me less cocky. I didn't know it at the time, but it also made me able to learn. I came back and told Pete what had happened. I was depressed and angry. Pete said, "Maybe God knows that you're not ready to get out. Instead of worrying about getting out, concentrate more on recovery. That will help you get ready to get out."

I spent a few more days locked in the cell. I thought about it. I knew he was right. I wanted to argue the point. But there just wasn't anyone to argue it with. I could not will my way out of prison. And I could not will away my alcoholism. My instinct to fight left. I gave way to surrender. I was assigned to work as Pete's inmate clerk. I was paid seven cents an hour. That was just enough to pay for my tobacco habit.

I got to know all our guest speakers. I listened to their stories. I grew to admire them. I remember one speaker— Rusty—in particular. Her husband, Bill, was an ex-con. He had served several years in Colorado prisons. When she spoke, more than 80 inmates went totally silent. I stood in the back of the room, next to the coffee pot. I was crying my eyes out. Rusty shared the tragedies she had put her son through while drinking. It reminded me of my own experiences. I had grown up with an alcoholic mother.

I also remember struggling with "the God thing." I couldn't believe that God had time for me. He had so many good Christians to attend to. Pete told me to pray about it. I probably did. Then one fall day, I was walking across the yard. I was going to work. For some reason, I was the only inmate going to work that morning. It was the day we turn clocks back for daylight savings time. It was nearly dark. It had been raining the night before. I noticed the deep, dark blue of the sky dotted with twinkling stars. Fresh, rain-scented mountain air filled my nostrils. Two blue jays flew overhead. On my left, I saw a huge green lawn with flowers. Beyond the prison fence, I watched a small cloud. It floated around a high mountain topped with snow.

Suddenly a feeling rose from deep in my heart. I knew God had made the deep blue of the sky. He had put that scent in the air. He had sent the blue jays that were flying over my head. He knew of every blade of grass and flower in that huge lawn. He made every tree and snowflake on the mountain. He made the cloud floating in the sky.

And He knew about me. To think that He didn't know about me was absurd. The knowledge of God shot through me like an arrow. I knew that from God, I had no secrets. God knew me better than I knew myself. And He still loved me!

Later, I told Pete about that morning. He said, "You've had a spiritual experience." I said, "Cool!" I read the Big Book. The part called "Spiritual Experience," Appendix II (page 567). And I knew it was true.

That was 17 years ago. Much has happened since then. I got out of prison. And though I haven't stayed sober the whole time, I now have 12 years. Most of that time was on the streets. Pete died, but I stayed very active in A.A. Except for one short stretch. And that's when life again became unmanageable. As a result, here I sit in prison today.

So there I was, all locked up safe and sound. Then I went back to that Grapevine article. Not long after that, I heard from Brian S. We've been writing now for a year. I consider him my sponsor. We share our experience, strength and hope through the mail. Recently he brought his family to Colorado on vacation. We drank coffee and talked in the prison visiting room. We talked for about an hour. Brian is an outstanding example of sobriety. The service he is doing is very important. I have come to believe this: Carrying the A.A. message to prisons is one of life's highest callings. There are 1.6 million prisoners in the United States. I believe most of their crimes involve alcohol or drugs. I believe this from firsthand experience. It would be easy to forget about them. We could leave treatment to the prison therapists and reformers. But, sadly, their programs are often useless.

But Alcoholics Anonymous offers a real solution. It can help the confused inmate and his or her family. A.A. offers a plan for living. It will keep us between the lines. But we must be willing to go to meetings and work with others. It not only helps us to live on the street. It helps us live in prison, too. And it treats the disease: the insanity of alcoholism. You can keep an alcoholic away from alcohol. But that does not deal with the problem. A.A. in prison does. Today my life has meaning and purpose. I, too, carry the message of A.A.

–Martin W., Limon, Colorado

NOT BAD FOR A REDNECK FROM MISSISSIPPI

I got sober on May 1, 1985. It was May Day in every sense of the word. I was crashing and burning. I was 21 years old and hell-bent on destroying myself.

I admire alcoholics who can walk in, right off the street, to a meeting. It takes guts. I was not one of those. I had to be told to go by a court. I had stayed six months at a recovery house in Mississippi. When I got out, I got to work. I dove into working the Twelve Steps. I went to as many A.A. meetings as I could. I had almost 14 months sober. Then, on June 26, 1986, I faced the judge. They were the charges that had landed me in the treatment center. A first offense: trying to sell drugs. I was sentenced to five years at the Mississippi State Department of Corrections in Parchman.

All my sober friends were shocked. I was too. How could God bring me this far just to abandon me? I was sent to a maximum facility lockdown. They put me with murderers, bank robbers, and other "real" criminals. Worse than that: I couldn't attend A.A. meetings for the first seven months. During that time, I picked and chopped cotton. I stood chest-deep in raw sewage as I worked on a blocked sewer line. I was raped many times. And I almost got drunk again.

Here's what kept me going: My sober friends would drive six hours every visiting Sunday. They would bring me an A.A. meeting. My immediate family never came to see me once. A.A. became my new family. Through them, I realized that my God had not left me. He was there in prison with me. He was also in the hugs, love, and support I got from my A.A. brothers and sisters. In between their visits, I read and read the Big Book. And I prayed for my safety so that I could get out alive. And sober.

I could easily have gotten drunk while in prison. Alcohol was easy to get. I guess I'm just lucky. I saw that I had a sober life, even as a prisoner. And it was better than being a prisoner of alcohol. Before I got sober, I just wanted to die. Sobriety had given me hope for a new life. I completed my sentence. When I walked out on parole, I was still sober.

Many amazing things have happened in my 16 sober years. There's been joy, and there's been tragedy. I was diagnosed with HIV the year I got sober. A few years later, the doctors found hepatitis C. I've often felt unlovable, less than, and alone. I've lost people I loved and cared for. I've had dreams broken, and dreams come true. I've traveled the world. I've gone to A.A. meetings in foreign lands: Prague, Rome, Jamaica, New Zealand, and Greece. I've reconnected with my family. I love them dearly. I have felt loved by them as well. I've written a book. I hope it will be published. I've had articles published in national magazines. I've had my songs set to music and recorded. I've carried the message by being a sponsor and a G.S.R. I've even been a keynote speaker at an A.A. convention. There were more than 3,000 people in the audience. Not bad for a dumb redneck from Mississippi!

But, mostly, I have come to believe. I have come to believe that things will work out for the best. As long as I don't drink. I believe that anything is possible. As long as I don't drink. I believe that I am a wonderful, loving man. A man full of life. And I have come to believe in a God who loves me, even though I have flaws. I owe it to having worked the Twelve Steps of Alcoholics Anonymous. I owe it to staying honest, open-minded, and willing. To performing service, and to being grateful. And I owe it, even during the dark times, to remembering this: Don't take that first drink, no matter what.

If you are thinking of taking a drink, think about this: It won't make it any better. Just don't drink today. You are worth it, whether you believe so or not. If you can't believe it, then believe that I believe it. I need every single one of you alcoholics out there. Wherever you may be, you help keep me full of hope. You help me live sober. Don't quit before the miracle!

—Jimmy W., Cazadero, California

ADDING UP
THE SCORE

A girl found A.A. in prison. She writes her "outside" sponsor a few weeks after her release.

Dear Georgiene:

I am going to write this. I hope it clears my mind as I write. I want to share these thoughts with you. You have just now received your present. It is an unopened half-pint of whiskey. I send it along with this letter.

As I write this letter, the bottle sits here. It is sitting on my dresser with my hair oil and cologne. It is the same color as my shampoo. And it means no more to me than my bottle of shampoo does.

It meant something to me when I bought it. I shook all over inside and out. I got that terrible pressure in my head again. I looked around outside the drugstore. I hoped no one had seen me. I felt so guilty. If a cop had tried to arrest me, I would have gone along willingly. I would have pleaded guilty. Of course, buying a bottle on Saturday night is not against the law. But it is against the "A.A. law." It is not God's will that I get drunk. It is against your principles and mine.

I bought it to prove something to myself. If I drank it,

I wanted to know how it would affect me. Would I have the DTs? Would I stay at home or go prowling? Would I get my novel out of my locked suitcase? I haven't read it or worked on it for months. Or would I come down to your apartment? Would I say, "Well, what do you think of me now? You are always telling me what a nice person I am and how much faith you have in me. What do you think of this?" Would I cry for Joe? Would I go to the bowling alley and look for Kenny? Would I ever be able to stop?

If I did not drink it, I wanted to know why. I am finding out now, as I write on this paper. I left it lying wrapped up and on the bed for 15 minutes. I ignored it. I fooled around cleaning up my closet. Then I took it out of the sack. I sat down on the chair and stared at it. I read the label. I thought: "Why, this little so-and-so! How could I let a little old bottle of liquid run my life? It is nothing. I am something. I am a human being. And I'm on the way to becoming a pretty darned good one. This bottle has power to make shaking cowards out of people. I can go it one better. I can beat it at its own game. I could go out right now. I could give those same people knowledge and power. I could show them how to never drink again as long as they live. I am the master here. And I say to hell with you!"

I got up and set it on the dresser. I turned on the overhead lamp. I let it shine full in my face. I looked in the mirror a long time. I saw the strain I had been under for the past week. I've had the flu and fever, and a swollen sinus. But I saw a lot more. I saw eyes that were bright and clear. They looked out at the world with good will and kindness. I saw the friendship of the A.A. members. It had made a great difference in the look on that face. Now the mouth looked like it could grin at any time. It used to be so grim and hard.

I sat down in a chair. I added up the score, the personal score. It goes like this:

1. Georgiene B. gave me more than sponsorship. She gave

me her friendship. She didn't have to. She did it because she likes me. She believes in me and really cares.

2. Elline M. is proud of me. She makes it a point to talk to me at the meetings. She invited me to her daughter's wedding. That is the best compliment I have ever had. I'll go, too.

3. Rosemary D. and I are forming a fine friendship.

4. Dean B. says keep up the good work and shakes my hand.

5. Charlie M. says I've "got A.A."

6. Alex V. singles me out to encourage me at meetings. He really likes me.

7. Margaret B. offered to share her home with me.

8. John H. enjoys my company.

9. Fran W. and Gene R. will be my friends as time marches on.

10. I can make a dream of Georgiene's come true. This should be the Number Two blessing on this list. I can go back to the Indiana Women's Prison as a speaker. I can be a sponsor and example. I can help the girls. I can help make up to Georgiene—for all her grief and heartaches over the last three years.

11. I was made head waitress after three weeks on my job. I am doing good work there.

12. I work hard. And on my one day off, I got up early. I went to Champaign, Illinois, to try and help Janie B.

13. I have attended three, four and five meetings a week, and six different A.A. groups. I do it to get the message as soon as possible. So I can be a good, working member and give back what I have received.

14. I have found out what Christian love is between people. Bishop Sheen talks about it all the time. But I couldn't believe in such a thing. Now I know.

15. I have taken the first seven of the Twelve Steps. I am letting God have His way with my life. He is doing a pretty good job.

16. I am happy in one room. My happiness has little to do with what I own.

This is the list of the best things that have been happening to me. They happened in the 31 days since my release from prison. How could I expect more? How could I handle any more right now?

Before I started this letter, I walked over to the closet to get my pajamas. All of a sudden I said, "Father, watch over me. Help me to do as You want me to do."

Georgiene, He did.

Your friend,
Dorothy
Indianapolis, Indiana

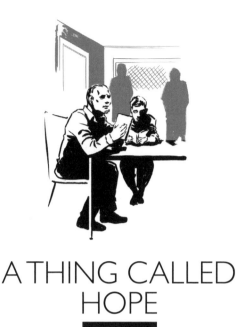

A THING CALLED HOPE

I am an alcoholic in prison. I am only 31 years of age. But I have been drinking for 19 years. I also began to use drugs shortly after my first drink. But I always have favored alcohol. Even when I was using another drug, alcohol was involved. This part of my story is like hundreds of others that I'm sure you have heard. I went through many short-lived jobs. I was kicked out of the worst of flophouses because of my drinking. At one point I used my welfare check to drink with. It was supposed to pay my rent.

This was insanity. It was the dead of winter in New York City. I had no friends or relatives to take me in. I made my home between the benches at the Astor Place and Broad Street subway stations. A cop would wake me at one bench and send me on my way. I would just head to my other home.

For the last 10 years of my drinking, everyone around me saw my problem. I had been arrested 72 times. Social workers at Welfare knew my problem. The judges and probation officers knew. They referred me to treatment programs. The programs all used A.A. as a tool. But "I was not an alcoholic." I resented them for thinking I was. I would not take that

First Step. And I never sobered up. I had been led to the water, but would not drink of it.

Each time I ended up in jail, it was usually for about 90 days. I would get out and head straight to the liquor store. But my freedom didn't last long. Every time I left jail, I knew I would be back again. It was only a question of how long.

In the last five years, I had come to believe that I was cursed. I tried to kill myself six times. I couldn't even do that right.

When I got to this prison, I began going to the A.A. meetings. I wanted to impress the parole board, and win an early release. Well, that didn't work. When I appeared before them, they "hit" me. The state wanted me to serve my full sentence.

Then something strange happened. A.A. had no chance of winning me an early release date. But I kept on going to meetings. Somewhere, somehow, somebody said something in one of those meetings. It gave me something I had never had before. Today I can name that something. It is called hope!

I heard people come in from outside and speak. These people had been as bad off as I was. Other speakers had not gotten that bad yet. Some had even been in prison before. But they all spoke of being happy today. I could tell that they were being honest. You could see the happiness all over their faces.

I decided that I wanted what they had. I got more involved. I began to read the Big Book, the Twelve and Twelve, *As Bill Sees It*, and *Alcoholics Anonymous Comes of Age*. Today I anxiously await each month's Grapevine—I have even managed to get about 200 back issues. They have become my favorite reading. Often when I read them, my eyes fill up with tears. I feel that new hope deep inside.

Today, I have a responsible job here in the prison. I am a counselor in the pre-release center. I have gotten an outside sponsor. He comes in once a week to visit me. He has been helping me work the Steps. I have put those Steps into my life. I have become an honest person. People are not afraid to trust or depend on me. I have even been elected chairman of our small meeting.

As I write this, I will complete my sentence in 66 days. I will be released. Today, I do not think, "How long will it be before I come back?"

The A.A. program has given me a sense of hope and peace. Even in a place like this. I want more of it when I get out. I have already chosen my first A.A. meeting. It is not too far from this prison. I know what I must do. It's what so many others before me have done. I must give away what was given so freely to me.

I thank all those wonderful A.A.s who came into this prison. I'm grateful for the message that they had to share with us.

—W.H., Bedford Hills, NY

FIVE SIMPLE ACTIONS

I poked my head in the doors of A.A. It was shortly after my second DUI. I wanted to put on a "game face" for the judge. I attended two meetings. I decided that I didn't need a dog-and-pony show. I could slip the conviction without it. I would sail away just fine. I ended up with a five-day sentence. I told my employer that I would need the week off for a family emergency. After the five days, I was released. The first thing I did was go to a bar to "buy a pack of cigarettes." For the next 10 years, I basically moved from one drink to the next.

My third DUI came as a tap on the shoulder by a local sheriff. He was concerned for my welfare. My car was halfway in my driveway, and halfway in the street. The motor was still running with the lights on. It was two hours after the bars had closed. I had passed out with my foot on the brake. When he asked me to put the car in park, it slipped into drive. I nearly ran him over.

Everyone at the bar swore by this one attorney. But I couldn't afford him. I settled for the lawyer handling my bankruptcy. She gave me a two-for-one special. I just asked that she get me off with house arrest. I thought I could not survive without a drink. I could get away with an ankle bracelet, and buy a keg on my way to work. She suggested that I start outpatient therapy right away. I swore I would. But I never got around to it.

I went in for the county pre-trial hearing. I had the usual "I'm a social drinker" song and dance. You know the routine: "Gosh, I really had no business driving that night. Boy, have I learned my lesson. Can I go home now?" I even bought a wallet. I could open it and show the photos of my two sons. I knew that would work.

I came before the judge. It didn't take very long. I saw that my bluff had been called. "I see a lot of red flags in your file," he said. "I can't tell you that you are an alcoholic. You have to decide that for yourself. But I'm going to give you some time to think about it." My heart dropped. He said, "I am sentencing you to one year in jail." He kept talking. But I couldn't hear the words. My mind was filled with one question: "How the hell am I going to drink?"

Afterwards, my lawyer told me that I had gotten a break. The judge had suspended 275 days of my sentence. I would probably serve around 60-70 days. "It really is not that bad," she said. Yeah. He also gave me two weeks to set my affairs in order. I briefly remember him saying, "There are meetings of Alcoholics Anonymous in the jail. I think that you should go to them."

I quickly filed my taxes. I paid my landlord three months' rent in advance. I had been dating a girl. It was only to use her car and booze. She said I had to stop drinking at once. I did my best to fool her for the next few weeks. That way she would continue to drive me around. Then came the day I had to turn myself in. The night before, she had wanted me to stay with her. But I told her that I needed to spend some time alone. I needed "quiet reflection." Could you believe that? I am about to lose every freedom I have. And the only thing I want to do is drink.

I had no clue what I was in for. The first two days, I was kept on 23-hour lockdown. I got to come out to eat meals. I was allowed only two books in my cell. My second trip to the book cart, I was just looking for a good read. I saw this little book with no title on the spine. It was blue. It was about the size of the other paperbacks. I picked it up. I saw the words pressed into the cover… *Alcoholics Anonymous.* "Damn," I thought. "There's that name again." I almost dropped it like a hot potato. But something happened. I realized where I was. Nobody gave a damn about me, much less what I read. I took it to my cell.

I wasn't really going to read it. I just peeled it open to any old page. I began skimming. I looked at the personal stories. I found that I had done most of the same things. I began to read deeper. The more I read, the more I thought: "I have something in common with these people." I think I also felt a bit of hope. I had been a bad man for a long time. But I had never been punished like this before. I was ashamed to be a prisoner.

Then they put me in with the other prisoners. I took my book with me. Other inmates told me how to get out fast: I needed to put my name in for trustee. And I had to be on my best behavior. I also saw a sign-up sheet at the guard's desk. It was for different programs. A.A. was one of them. I signed up for A.A. I thought A.A. would earn me some brownie points. It would help me get placed in a work program.

I went to the meetings every Tuesday and Thursday. I listened, and I understood. I even began "sharing," but it was more like a rant. I began to see this: Nearly everyone in jail was there because of alcohol or drugs. I also saw that we all are very selfish. We're also self-destructive, to the point of being insane. If someone else had hurt me the way I hurt myself, I would have hunted him down. I saw that my best thinking got me where I was. My way landed me in jail. Maybe I don't really know what's best for me after all. Maybe the

Sunday Suits were right all along. Maybe it was time to try someone else's way. My way didn't work anymore.

I also noticed the jail's mirrors. You don't have a real mirror. Not like at home to comb your hair or shave. It's more like a piece of stainless steel bolted to the wall. It looks like someone cleaned it with sandpaper. You couldn't see yourself very well. That was okay. I never much cared to look myself in the eye anyhow. But I saw that I had a pretty blurry image of myself.

After about six weeks there, something happened to me. There was a big game on that night. I had the "throne"—the seat right under the television set. This was no ordinary game either. My hockey team was going to stay alive or die in the Stanley Cup playoffs. About the same time the puck dropped, the guard got on the horn. He said, "Anybody signed up for that A.A. meeting, time to go!" I thought to myself, "Hell, those guys will be here next Tuesday. So will I. I'm not missing this game. I'm not giving up this seat for anything." Just as fast as I had that thought, another one raced through my head: "I'd better get up off my butt. I'd better try and get what A.A. has to offer. If I don't, I'll have a lot of time to watch games in jail." I got up and went to the meeting.

I knew something had changed. But I didn't say anything to anyone. I was afraid I would jinx it. I just kept going to the meetings. I kept reading the book. The guys who brought the meetings to us gave me a book of the meetings on the outside. They told me that when I got out, I'd have two choices: go to a meeting, or go to the bar.

The day I got out, I went to a meeting. I walked in feeling pretty high and mighty. I was cocky about my days of sobriety. I was ready to announce my sober time. And do it to a group I'd never met. They could fight over who gets to sponsor me. I had a speech all memorized.

After listening to a few people talk, I realized that it was different "on the outs." I began to feel nervous. I waited for a pause in the sharing. Then I nearly barfed out my speech: "Hi my name is Tony…and I just got out of jail…and I'm looking for a sponsor…and if anybody wants to be my sponsor…please talk to me after the meeting…Thhhhanks." It didn't go over as well as I had planned. But it did break the ice. The guy next to me started talking. He sounded really familiar. I looked at him. His face was familiar.

After the meeting, he turned to me. He said, "Just got out of jail, huh?" "Uh huh." "Who was your judge?" he asked. "Um, you were," I said. "What's it feel like to be face to face with the guy who put you in jail?" he asked. To this day, I don't know where this came from, but I said, "It's tough. I have to deal with it every morning in the mirror."

They told me I would never have to drink again. They would show me how. I follow the suggestions as best I can. Some days are better than others. But I now have over 1,200 days of sobriety. The obsession is gone. I am by no means perfect. I still go through all kinds of issues. But I don't have to drink over them. I go to meetings. I have a sponsor. I take the Steps. I help others. And I hit my knees.

You may hear lots of people speak about "working" the Steps. But that isn't entirely accurate. "Work" was trying to get from one drink to the next. "Work" was trying to fool people. Being a practicing alcoholic was "work." This is freedom. Freedom from a prison. One I was in long before it had walls that I could touch.

—Tony F., Parker, Colorado

ERNEST C., THE COFFEEPOT AND ME

Here is how I met Ernest C. and found A.A. I think old Ernest would enjoy hearing this little story.

In 1986, I'd spent six years at the state prison in Reidsville. I was transferred to the old Buford rock quarry prison. At Buford, I was into the same kind of stuff as Reidsville. Only it was easier for me to get into trouble.

Most people think that prison will stop you from doing wrong. But doing wrong is a lifestyle. In prison, you just learn more wrong. And how to get away with it better. Everyone around you has gotten busted. They tell you how not to get busted. So that is something you learn in prison.

I had been at Buford a few months. Then someone asked me to go to A.A. with him. He said that an old man came every Saturday. He brought coffee and stuff to eat. He passed out cigarettes. I was also told he had a big wooden box. He kept his coffeepot in it. He had sugar as well. I had to look into this.

I forgot to tell you something: I'm an alcoholic. I was locked up in 1980. Since then, I spent most of my time thinking of ways to stay high. Everyone knew me as "the man with the high." No one could stop me. No matter where they put me. No matter how much time they spent watching me. Drinking was my life.

I remember the first time I saw Ernest C. He was standing in a visiting room full of convicts. He was telling them that he was there because he loved them. I used to hear people say, "I love you." I'd always say to myself, "I'd better keep an eye on them. They want something."

So I sat there at the back of the room. I was drinking coffee and smoking cigs. I was looking for the box that kept all that sweet sugar. I needed that sugar. And I needed a big coffeepot to do my cooking in. I could almost taste the buck (bootleg booze).

After the meeting, Ernest C. put his things away. He said something about "Keep coming back. It works." I said to myself, "This old man is nuts." I figured something had to be wrong with him. No one comes to a prison and says stuff like "I love you, boys. Keep coming back. It works." Man, he was on something that I never had. (I was right about that.)

The next week I got into the box. I took out the pot and sugar. I made me some good old buck. One cup and a small joint. I was in heaven.

This went on until I got so drunk I couldn't walk. Then an officer found Ernest C.'s coffeepot. It smelled like something had died in it. They took me to the hold for 28 days. I had been there before. And I would be back. That goes with the lifestyle.

I did my time in the hold. I was sent back to the dorm. Well, here comes Saturday again. I was looking out the window. Old Ernest C. came pulling up. Others told me that he had to get another pot. I felt bad, but I didn't let it show.

The call came for the A.A. meeting. I didn't even think about going. And I sure didn't want to hear what Ernest C. had to say to me.

I heard the officer at the door calling my name. I had a buddy of mine go to the door. He told the officer that I wasn't going to A.A. So he could stop calling my name. Well, that didn't work. My buddy came back. He said those words I'd heard before: "They want to talk to you."

I said, "Let me get this over with. I'll be right back." The officer said, "They want you in the superintendent's office." When I went in, Ernest C. was standing there. He was smiling. He looked right at me. He said, "How was your vacation?" I said, "Pretty bad. No sun at all." He said, "Let me ask you something. I need someone to come in and make the coffee. Someone to set up for the meetings on Saturday. I also need someone to keep up with the pot. And all the other stuff I bring. To let me know when I need to bring more." He reached out and handed me a key to the box.

I almost fell over right there in front of him and the superintendent. The superintendent said, "If you want to do it, you can." So I took the key. I was lost for the way I was feeling inside.

That night, I walked into the meeting. No one said anything. I had messed up. But no one was getting on my case about it. That was something new to me. There was Ernest C. He was back up there, saying those words again: "I'm here tonight, boys, because I love you." After the meeting he said, "Keep coming back. It works."

That was 14 years ago. My life has changed so much. A.A. and people like Ernest C. have become my way of life. Whenever I get a chance, I stand up in front of people. I say these words: "I'm here tonight because God loved me. He sent Ernest C. and the program of A.A. into my life. I love y'all. Keep coming back. It works."

P.S. Ernest C. is still taking meetings into prison. Because he loves the men and women there. And he wants them to find a new way of life.

—Marshall M., Hancock State Prison, Georgia

COMING HOME

I am writing this letter from the Billerica House of Corrections. It's in Billerica, Massachusetts. I'm serving a six-month sentence for my third drunk-driving conviction.

I'm not a typical inmate here. I've never had any problems with the law. Only my drunk-driving arrests. No one in my family has ever spent time in prison. So I'm the first. I'm married and own a house. I pay taxes and have a good paying job. I have a college education. I'm a graduate student at a college in Boston. I'm studying for my Master of Fine Arts in creative writing. But alcohol doesn't care about any of these things. In here, I'm just another convict who broke the law.

Still, I consider myself very lucky. I attended my first A.A. meeting the night after my arrest. That was nearly six months before I went to prison. I'm grateful that I didn't have to go any lower. I was willing to surrender. I was blessed: I came into prison with six months of sobriety and the A.A. program.

I received my "gift of desperation" when I woke up in the holding cell. It was in the police station the morning of my arrest. This gift came right away. I said to myself, "I've done it

106

again. I swore I'd never drink and drive again. But I've done just that." I felt sick inside. I knew that I'd let down my wife and my family. Also my friends and myself. And I'd put other people's lives in danger.

This was the insanity of my disease. I would do things drunk that I'd never do when I was sober. I finally admitted it to myself: I was powerless over alcohol. My life had been unmanageable for a long time. That's when the miracle of my recovery began.

I went to my first A.A. meeting. It was in the town where my wife and I lived at the time. As soon as I entered the room, a man introduced himself. He asked me if this was my first time at A.A. (How did he know that?) He got me a cup of coffee. He found me a place to sit. A woman joined me soon afterwards. Both of these kind, friendly people stayed with me the whole meeting. They made me feel warm and welcome. These people are now two of my best friends in A.A. I'm proud to say that.

There's a story in the Big Book called "Women Suffer Too." The author talks about the Old Testament. The Hebrew word for "salvation" means "to come home to one's own kind." That's the way I felt the moment I walked into that first meeting. I was home with my own kind at last. Probably for the first time in my adult life.

For the next five and a half months, I attended meetings every day. I went to more than one meeting a day when possible. I joined a number of groups. I found a sponsor. I listened to his suggestions. I talked to everyone I could talk to, both going to and from meetings. I stuck out my hand. I asked for people's phone numbers.

I'd been sober for three months. I started going on speaking commitments with my groups. I shared my story with others. Throughout this time, the court kept delaying my case. That added to the fear I felt. I talked about this fear with my sponsor and my friends in A.A. They all advised me to "turn it over" to God. Let Him handle it for me. This was a new idea for me. It took a lot of practice. Then I began to feel a change. I kept turning my will and my life over to God. The process slowly became second nature to me. It was the best way to handle my fear and doubt. Whether in my court case, or any other situation.

I finally went to trial for my drunk-driving case. My A.A. friends were there. They gave moral support to my wife and me. The judge praised my efforts to turn my life around. Then he sentenced me to jail. I would pay for my mistakes. I would begin to clear away the wreckage of my past. These same A.A. friends comforted my wife. They promised to help her out while I was gone. They would make sure she was okay.

My sponsor and my A.A. friends visit me whenever they can. They tell me I'm in their prayers. I've learned to pray, thanks to A.A. I thank God for putting all these wonderful people in my life. I also ask Him to remove my obsession and desire for alcohol. This conscious contact with God is an enormous comfort to me. I've never before had it in my life. I was spiritually bankrupt when I drank. I saw this when my father passed away. It was nine months before my coming into A.A.

I know that I don't have to be alone any longer. For that I'm grateful. The Big Book tells me: "I came to A.A. solely for the purpose of sobriety, but it has been through A.A. that I found God."

During my time in prison, I've missed my regular meetings. I've missed my friends from those meetings. But I never forget all that I've learned from them. I am with these friends in thought and spirit. Every night I think of what meeting I would be going to. I see it in my mind. I see the people who attend that meeting. In this simple way, I feel I'm with my friends.

Here in prison we have two meetings a week. The inmates run both of them. It helps them earn "good time." I try to share often. There aren't many speakers. I either tell my story or I read a chapter from the Big Book. Or I may read a story from Grapevine. My wife sends me each new issue of Grapevine. It's a wonderful feeling when I receive it. I try to share my experience, strength, and hope with other inmates. I always hope it will plant the seed, or help someone who wants sobriety. I also know this helps keep me sober.

I look forward to getting out of prison in four or five months. I want to get back to the new life that I left behind. I hope to continue working my program of recovery. I hope I can become the person I always wanted to be. I want to be a husband, brother, son, friend, and employee that people can be proud of. I hope to share my experience in prison with others. Maybe I can help someone avoid the mistakes I made. I believe that God has given me a second chance. He has let me see with new eyes. I see all those special things in my life that I took for granted. God willing, I'll have a life that is second to none. One day at a time. And I will never have to see the inside of these prison walls again.

—Keith C., Billerica, Massachusetts

JUMP RIGHT IN

My name is Glenn R. I grew up in Randallstown, Maryland. It's now a major suburb of Baltimore. But when I was young, it was a small town. I played Pop Warner football and baseball. I was very good. I got a big head at a young age.

When I was 12, I slept over at a friend's house one Friday night. I was shocked. His parents left their supply of liquor right out in the open. I had never drunk alcohol before. I'd never really had the chance. I asked my friend if I could have some drinks. He told me that he didn't care. I quickly took my first drinks. I started to feel warm and then dizzy. I threw up all over the floor. My friend was great. He cleaned it up. He figured that I had learned my lesson.

But I was hooked. I decided to get more alcohol. I started hanging out in front of the liquor store. I hoped to see friends of my older brother. They could get me some beer. I did this several times. Then my brother found out. He strong-armed his mates. He told them not to help me.

My Pop Warner football team won two national titles. My opinion of myself grew. By age 16, I was going to the local bar. I was ordering whiskey and cola chasers. I thought I was so cool. I didn't care about anybody else. I got my driver's license. My grandmother gave me a car. Within two weeks, I wrecked it.

The police sent me to my first alcohol classes. They also sent me to A.A. meetings. At the classes, they showed pictures of dead people. They had been killed in car accidents. Some had their heads cut off. But that didn't really bother me. It started my pattern: I would do anything to get back to the drink. I did what the law told me to do. I did what my parents and teachers said. They were all satisfied. Then I started to sell illegal drugs.

Things really started to get worse. My baseball batting average went from .406 to .320. My drinking took more and more control of my life. I got myself into deep trouble with the police, and they questioned me right in my parent's living room. I was released but they said I would be contacted. I was ashamed being alone with my parents. I knew that I was guilty in their eyes. In the past, I was always able to make excuses for my actions. But I could not this time.

I was put on probation. I was under orders to attend college. I had to see some counselors. I convinced them that I was going to be all right. It worked for over a year. Then I started drinking again. I flunked out of college.

I met my future wife. She helped me to get a good job. It was with a major chemical company. It was wonderful making lots of money. But it pushed me to drink. For the next 15 years, I drank whenever I could. I drank to cover my pain. My marriage had failed. My life was a failure. I had all the chances to solve my alcoholism. But I always thought I would die drunk.

I lost my job due to drinking. I was put into treatment for alcoholism and depression. I stayed sober for eight months. Then I told myself that I needed a few beers to relax. I had landed a job with the post office. I thought I was doing okay. I thought I was controlling my drinking. But slowly "the control" started to slip away. My "control" was only a dream. I went to a Christmas party at a bar in Gulfport, Florida. They offered free drinks for an hour. I downed four very powerful Bloody Marys. I went into a blackout. I drove 90 miles an hour on a city street in St. Petersburg. I didn't even know it.

I thought the police car was an ambulance. I had pulled over to let them by. Then I realized they were police. They were going to arrest me. I freaked out and started driving away. The policeman dove through the car window. We fought until he fell out of the car. This happened as I was driving 40 miles per hour. By the grace of God, he was not seriously hurt. I then ran 13 stop signs at over 90 miles per hour. I apparently saw a road block with flashing lights. I thought of running full speed into them. But I didn't. By the grace of God, I surrendered to everything.

I was sentenced to 25 months in Florida prison. With good behavior, I served 21½ months.

While in prison, I went to A.A. meetings whenever possible. I was blessed to have a Big Book. I read the chapter, "There is a Solution" more than 90 times. I really needed to grasp that fact: there was a solution to my drinking.

When I was near the end of my prison time, I wrote the head office of A.A. in New York. I asked for a person to contact in St. Petersburg. John M. wrote me. He sent information on A.A. And he sent a number to call when I got out. When the time came, I made that phone call.

John came right over. He became my temporary sponsor. He took me to A.A. meetings. He gave me a local meeting schedule. He even helped me to find a job. He was great. I am blessed. I kept going to meetings. I've become involved with other wonderful A.A. people.

My A.A. home group votes each week on a spiritual principle. We might take the principle of "unselfishness," for example. Then we practice it during the week, one day at a time. Then we come back to our home group. And we share our experience, strength and hope through practicing the principle. This helps us to learn and live A.A. I also like getting to my home group early. Then I can make the coffee.

I have received love and support from those in my home group. I found it also in other meetings I attend. It amazes me. My isolation from people had always been based on fear. But today, I know a new life with the God of my understanding. A.A. led me to a personal relationship with my Higher Power. I choose to call that Power God. I love A.A. I know it has saved my life.

—Larry P., St. Petersburg, Florida

LIFE IS GOOD

I am like a lot of women in prison. I was a victim of sexual assault. It also started my 23-year drinking career. My youth and innocence were taken from me. Along with every ounce of self-esteem I had. Which wasn't much to begin with. I got angry at God. How could He let such bad things happen to good people? Instead of turning to God for help, I turned away. I turned to alcohol. I found a new life with drinking. I found new friends. And I felt like I belonged somewhere again.

I had been raised in a good home. I had good parents. I lied to my family to keep my secret. I didn't want to hurt them. My lifestyle changed. I had been a "good kid." But I started sneaking out to bars when I was underage. I became immoral. I did not care about anyone else but myself. I was always looking for something. Maybe I wanted my self-esteem back. I'm not sure. But I tried to find it in alcohol and men, any man.

In my early 20s, I looked at my lifestyle. I could see myself still sitting on that barstool when I was 60. I was afraid I would live like this the rest of my life. I figured there was only one way out: Get married and settle down. I settled down for a while. He didn't. The marriage ended six years later. One good thing came out of the marriage: my son. When the marriage ended I returned to my first love. That was alcohol.

I drank for over 20 years. That led to drug abuse and dealing. That led to my arrest five years ago. More than a few S.W.A.T. members paid me a visit. They had a "no knock" warrant. I was released that first night. But I didn't take their advice very seriously. I went right back to what I was doing before. So they paid me another visit. This time, I saw they were serious.

At the first arrest, they took my son from me. Thankfully, I was able to get him back. At the next arrest, I wasn't so lucky. I'll never forget having those assault rifles pointed at our heads. They took my son away to foster care. Then began the court dates. As I look back now, I can't believe how arrogant I was. I thought, "I've just made some mistakes over the years. This isn't really who I am. They can't possibly send me to prison." Wrong.

At the time I was involved in a relationship. It was not a healthy one. I was also pregnant with twins. So here I am: My son is gone. I'm pregnant and facing prison. And I'm scared to death. How did my life get so out of control? What happened to me? I was miserable. I had hit bottom. I decided to do something I hadn't done in years. I decided to pray. I talked to the God of my childhood.

I found the only quiet place in the house. It was a closet. I poured my heart and soul out to the God I knew years before. He listened. I don't remember much of what happened after the prayer. I just know I had a great sense of peace. That was something I hadn't felt for a while. I asked God to please keep me out of prison. But that wasn't the plan God had in mind. In April, I was sentenced to the Utah Department of Corrections. At my sentencing, I prayed, "God, if I have to go to prison, please come with me." He did.

In prison, God led me to A.A. I started going to meetings. I did it to get out of my cell for an hour. It was something to fight the boredom. But as I listened, I realized they were talking about me. For years, I had told myself I was "a good person who had made bad choices." But that wasn't true. I was an alcoholic.

God and A.A. became my lifeline. It's how I made it through. For the rest of my two years in prison, I attended A.A. faithfully. People carried the message of A.A. into the prison system. They saved my life. I had my beautiful twin daughters in prison. That was one of the hardest things I've ever gone through. I had my daughters on August 2. Five days later, I was released from the hospital. They sent me back to prison. I didn't see my daughters again for 16 months.

But I did one thing right. It was because I found God and A.A. in prison. I took my daughters with me when I was released. I found an A.A. home group right away. I had to learn to live on the streets, without alcohol. Working the Twelve Steps taught me how to do that.

I had relationships to mend with family. Most of all, I had to reunite with my son. God saw fit to give me custody of him again. My daughters, too. I made amends to my son. He was now 13. It was one of the most frightening things I have ever done. But he was very forgiving. I earned his trust. And the trust of the rest of my family. It took time. But it was well worth it. My children and I now have a loving relationship. My brothers and sisters have welcomed me back. I also made amends to myself. I learned how to forgive myself for all the pain I caused others. A.A. taught me how to forgive myself. But it also helped me find something else. I like myself.

I still have struggles in life. Who doesn't? But now, I work the Twelve Steps in all of life's struggles. I no longer use alcohol for answers, or to dull the pain. Life is good, thanks to God and A.A.

—Diane F., Perry, Utah

THE TWELVE STEPS OF
ALCOHOLICS ANONYMOUS

1. We admitted we were powerless over alcohol—that our lives had become unmanageable.

2. Came to believe that a Power greater than ourselves could restore us to sanity.

3. Made a decision to turn our will and our lives over to the care of God *as we understood Him.*

4. Made a searching and fearless moral inventory of ourselves.

5. Admitted to God, to ourselves, and to another human being the exact nature of our wrongs.

6. Were entirely ready to have God remove all these defects of character.

7. Humbly asked Him to remove our shortcomings.

8. Made a list of all persons we had harmed, and became willing to make amends to them all.

9. Made direct amends to such people wherever possible, except when to do so would injure them or others.

10. Continued to take personal inventory and when we were wrong promptly admitted it.

11. Sought through prayer and meditation to improve our conscious contact with God *as we understood Him,* praying only for knowledge of His will for us and the power to carry that out.

12. Having had a spiritual awakening as the result of these steps, we tried to carry this message to alcoholics, and to practice these principles in all our affairs.

THE TWELVE TRADITIONS OF
ALCOHOLICS ANONYMOUS

1. Our common welfare should come first; personal recovery depends upon A.A. unity.

2. For our group purpose there is but one ultimate authority—a loving God as He may express Himself in our group conscience. Our leaders are but trusted servants; they do not govern.

3. The only requirement for A.A. membership is a desire to stop drinking.

4. Each group should be autonomous except in matters affecting other groups or A.A. as a whole.

5. Each group has but one primary purpose—to carry its message to the alcoholic who still suffers.

6. An A.A. group ought never endorse, finance, or lend the A.A. name to any related facility or outside enterprise, lest problems of money, property, and prestige divert us from our primary purpose.

7. Every A.A. group ought to be fully self-supporting, declining outside contributions.

8. Alcoholics Anonymous should remain forever non-professional, but our service centers may employ special workers.

9. A.A., as such, ought never be organized; but we may create service boards or committees directly responsible to those they serve.

10. Alcoholics Anonymous has no opinion on outside issues; hence the A.A. name ought never be drawn into public controversy.

11. Our public relations policy is based on attraction rather than promotion; we need always maintain personal anonymity at the level of press, radio, and films.

12. Anonymity is the spiritual foundation of all our traditions, ever reminding us to place principles before personalities.